Shaped
by
Pain

ISBN 978-1-952320-93-4 (Paperback)
Shaped by Pain
Copyright © 2020 Riel Pasaribu

Yorkshire Publishing
1425 E 41st Pl
Tulsa, OK 74105
www.YorkshirePublishing.com
918.394.2665

Printed in the USA

Shaped
by
Pain

Better Not Bitter

Riel Pasaribu

T U L S A

CONTENTS

Dedicated to
All airplane crash and burn survivors

PROLOGUE

Afflictions, trials, storms, tribulations, wildernesses, and diseases bring *pain*. Nobody wants to welcome pain, and there is no absolute way to get rid of it. Pain is not welcome, but it must be addressed. Pain is not an enjoyable circumstance. It can bring stress and even destroy your life. Pain does not choose whom to afflict or when to afflict. It does not ask your permission nor identify who you are. It comes to the rich and the poor. It hits the strong and the weak. Pain is not a respecter of a person. It attacks you suddenly or slowly. Pain is around us, whether it is physical, emotional, or spiritual. You never know or understand why it happens. The Scriptures remind us about it: "The thief comes only to steal and kill and destroy; I have come that they may have life and have it to the full (John 10:10)[1]." Stealing, killing, and destroying are all the works of the devil to make your life a less-than-gratifying, unhappy, boring, or unimportant life. But Jesus says, "I am come that they might have life, and that they might have it more abundantly (John 10:10)."

What a comparison! The devil comes to steal, to kill, and to destroy, but Jesus comes to give life as we have never known it! In your walk, you will experience times when the devil pushes buttons in your emotions to keep you all bound up and depressed. It is obvious that God does not afflict you, but Satan does—even though God can sometimes allow affliction to happen for His own purposes and reasons.

Pain has a scale. When you visit your physician, he or she will ask you the level of your pain: "On a scale of 1 to 5, what is the level of your pain?" The level of your pain will determine what kind of treatment you are going to receive, and your physician will work up to the level of your pain to overcome it. The physicians themselves do not feel your pain, but you do. Therefore, the healing is your choice. Do you decide to be healed or to stay in your pain? The decision is in your hands. Your medicine is in there, and at the appointment time, your doctor is ready to take care of you. Are you in pain? How painful is it? Do you become bitter or better because of it? Are you ready to face it? The decision is up to you.

If you have pain, you are not alone; I am with you and I have been there. You currently often hear the term, 'fake news.' My friend, this is my real story. I was an airplane crash survivor. I was afflicted with burns on 50 percent of my body, and I went through a near-death experience. The horrible accident nearly took my life. However, the strong hand of God snatched me away from that horrifying accident.

Read this book and you will see how I become better, and not bitter, because of the pain that afflicted me. Likewise, if you went through pain—in fact, if you are having pain right now—you can be better and not bitter. Your afflictions and storms are not all wasted. God is with you in your pain, and He is never surprised by it. Unlike the physician in the hospital that visits you only on a certain hour, my Great Physician is around all the time without an appointment. He is ready to turn around your trials to become your triumphs, and your test to become your testimony. Your pain will not last long; it is only temporary. Do not end your life permanently over a temporary storm. You don't need to end your life to end your pain. We all experience pain. Nevertheless, God promises that there is a purpose in all pain. It is an instrument to shape you for your better life. Are you in pain? Please do not give up. You can be whole again and become a better person!

ACKNOWLEDGMENTS

If God is around, then there would be no tragedy, because God is omnipotent, omniscient, and omnipresent. God holds the world in the palm of His hand. Therefore, if the tragedy happened, it is because God was absent. In other words, tragedy is the absence of God. This is the conclusion of some people when tragedy and storms suddenly attack. If God so loves the people whom He created, then pain should not be a part of human beings' lives—otherwise He is not a loving God. Pain has made many people become bitter and turn their backs on God. On the other hand, many people become better and stronger because of pain. You read in the Bible about many people who experienced a turnaround and who were used by God mightily after going through tribulations, like Job, David, and Paul. That being said, it is possible to experience a turning point in life. It is not the plan of God to pull you down; rather, it is His delight to pull you up from the mud that buried you deep, and to make you ready to stand up one more time for a better life.

This book not only shows you how many people have made it, but I will show you how I made it. *Shaped by Pain* is not only experienced by other people, but pain truly shaped my life. Through pain, God not only rejuvenated my physical body, but God rejuvenated my soul, and I was able to claim and proclaim my victory in Christ. My scars do not show who I am. I am not defined by the scars on my body. In fact, they are beautiful scars that are used by God to beautify my soul—it was broken, but it is a beautiful broken now.

Afflicted with burns on 50 percent of my body, going through a near-death experience, hospitalized for six months, and having to stay at home for eight more months was a horrible experience and a real pain.

Remembering those dark days, my words could not express my gratitude to my Protector and Healer, Jesus Christ. With all confidence, I can say that I was restored by the touch of God. His grace and compassion that healed me are beyond my understanding. I also recognize that there were many people around me who prayed for my healing. I did not stand alone in my story. Many people contributed to it. I thank many medical doctors, especially my burn doctor and orthopedist. To many friends who showed sympathy and who supported me in prayer, I owe a great debt of gratitude. To my boys, Timothy, Daniel, Joshua, and Jonathan, who had been away from me for many months: I thank you for your patience to wait for Dad to return home. I thank my beautiful wife, who nursed me at home and patiently waited

for my long recovery. Finally, I give all glory and honor only to Jesus Christ, my Savior and Lord.
Blessings,

Dr. Riel Pasaribu
Pickerington, Ohio
August 2020
riel.pasaribu@yahoo.com

Chapter 1

WISHING LIFE WOULD BE GOING SMOOTHLY

"For my thoughts are not your thoughts, neither are your ways my ways," declares the LORD. "As the heavens are higher than the earth, so are my ways higher than your ways and my thoughts than your thoughts."
(Isaiah 55:8-9)

Nobody wants a storm in life. We send "a happy trip," "wishing a safe flight and peaceful journey" to someone whom we love. Everybody wishes for a smooth flight in the air, and for calm sailing on the sea without turbulence or storm. Yes, all of us would like to enjoy a safe drive on land, a smooth flight in the air, and calm cruising on the sea. We do not want a disturbing moment. But many times, though, we can feel the turbulence in the air and the storm on the sea. The violent or unsteady movement of air and the strong winds on the sea have caused turbulence.

As an airplane crash victim, I do not like turbulence during my flight. Due to my past experience, turbulence makes me nervous. When the airplane that I was on crashed, leaving many people dead and burned, including me with burns on 50 percent of my body, I was left in bad trauma. The trauma was so severe that every time I fly, I wish that I could fly without any turbulence in the air. Reality is not that way; in a moment, the blue sky could turn to a cloudy sky and cause turbulence. We are delighted to see a blue sky, because it indicates confidence and stability, but we do not like dark clouds, because they represent the stormy situations in our lives. However, even a clear blue sky does not exempt turbulence. One day I flew over Tokyo, heading to Indonesia, in a clear blue sky—suddenly, though, the airplane shook violently and made me nervous. Nobody likes turbulence, storms, or turmoil. Everybody wishes that their days will be full of joy and blessing.

In America, almost every day we can hear everybody wishing us to have a good day. Or you can hear your Christian fellows saying, "Wishing you to have a good morning," or "Wishing you to have a blessed day." What is a blessed day? I guess that your fellow man wishes you a day free from sickness, conflict, hardship, trouble, and tribulation. These wishes are acts of prayer and hope. There is nothing wrong with having hope in God that He may make everything smoothly and beautifully done in our lives. However, our blessed day today is not because of the wishes of friends—it is because of God's goodness and grace that our days are blessed. Therefore, even without the approval of friends or other people wishing us,

"Have a blessed day," God will bless our day because God is a good God. The act of God does not depend on our wishes. In the same way, if we have pain and suffering today, it is not because some friends did not pray for us or say, "Have a blessed day," or "Have a nice one." Rather, it is because God allows us to go through pain and suffering.

Pain and suffering exist and are inevitable, just like a blessed day is inevitable. Just as many people were blessed with many newborn babies, many other people were broken with the losses of their babies. The ratio is still the same: one was born, and one died. Timothy Keller puts it this way, "Tens of thousands of people die every day in unexpected tragedies, and hundreds of thousands around them are crushed by grief and shock. The majority of them trigger no headlines because pain and misery is the norm in this world.[1]" Timothy Keller goes on to say, "Many times we think to ourselves that such things only happen to other people, to the poor, or to people who do not take precautions. Or we tell ourselves that if only we get the right people into the office and get our social systems right, nothing like this will happen again. The fact is, suffering is everywhere, unavoidable, and its scope often overwhelms[2]."

It is hard, and sometimes impossible, to fathom the ways of God within our human limitation. Paul, the apostle who went through many trials and sufferings, expressed it humbly: "Oh, how great are God's riches and wisdom and knowledge! How impossible it is for us to understand his decisions and his ways! (Rom 11:33)." Paul acknowledges the mystery of God, and Paul expects to not understand God's ways. No matter how hard we work to prevent pain and trials, our human ability is subject to the ways and wisdom of God. God knows better what is going on in this world that He created. God knows better about us than we know ourselves. Therefore, God knows what is happening to us. God created human beings according to His image, and He put His attributes into them. But not His powers of omnipotence, omniscience, and omnipresence. We will never be equal with God. He reigns on His own terms and, therefore, He exercises His sovereignty throughout the world.

Socrates, the first philosopher, once said, "I know one thing: that I know nothing."[3] How can a great philosopher and one of the smartest men on earth know nothing? Socrates was right; he was maybe the smartest person in his time, but he knew nothing, especially about tomorrow. He might have been endowed with high intelligence, but he was too limited to know the plan of God about his tomorrows. Due to the limitations of human beings to predict what is going to happen in the future, no wonder King Solomon wrote: "Do not boast about tomorrow, for you do not know what a day may bring (Prov 27:1)." James might have thought of this verse when he wrote, "While you don't know what will happen tomorrow. What is the meaning of your life? Your life is like a vapor that briefly appears and then vanishes (James 4:14)." Because of the shortness and uncertainty of life, all our plans must always depend on what God wants, and not on our own assumptions (James 4:15).

This truth about the uncertainty of the future applies to the need always to trust in the One who holds our tomorrows. The verse rules out one's overconfident sense of ability to control the future. No one can presume that the future will go smoothly or be stable. Wishing a smooth journey for Israel in the desert was a mere dream. The Bible recounts that the journey in the wilderness was full of hardships, trials, and suffering. Testing was inevitable when Israel walked in the desert for forty years before they arrived in the Promised Land.

Walking in the Rough Way

We organize things well to help achieve goals smoothly. Staying organized and planning makes things easier. Staying organized is not always a breeze, but we still want to make plans to assure that everything we do will not go roughly. I believe that making a good plan will produce a good result. Solomon expresses this when he says, "The plans of the diligent lead to profit as surely as haste leads to poverty (Prov 21:5)." Plans lead to profit. Therefore, a plan is very important in every area of life.

When you make the right plan, then there is a possibility of harvesting a profit. Thank God for the wisdom of planning and organizing to get things well done as planned. But why do our plans often go wrong? Is a plan not enough to smooth out all the roads and to guarantee success? To some people, a plan could be everything. Therefore, they solely depend on their plan. However, to some, a plan is only a limited tool. Indeed, "No matter how well we have put together a good life, no matter how hard we have worked to be healthy, wealthy, comfortable with friends and family, and successful with our career—something will inevitably ruin it. No amount of money, power, and planning can prevent bereavement, dire illness, relationship betrayal, financial disaster, or a host of other troubles from entering your life."[2]

Solomon, a man of wisdom and the richest man described in the Bible, reminds us of the involvement of God, the Great Planner, in every area of life. Solomon puts it this way, "The heart of man plans his way, but the Lord establishes his steps" (Prov 16:9 ESV).

I used to have a stable life, and I enjoyed it. I lived a normal life and I did normal stuff. Working in a different city required me to fly to the city where I worked. Reaching my workplace as planned, and doing work as planned, would be a normal routine for me. I assume, as a believer, that you want to pray that God will give you a safe and peaceful flight every time you make a trip. I am with you—and I prayed, trusting God that I would reach my workplace safe, and would do my routine work on that day. I planned to go to my workplace, and not to the hospital. However, I ended up in the hospital for six months, and I never got back to my office after that. My plan to live a smooth life was shattered. I was crushed severely. The airplane crash nearly took my life. I was in trouble, and I was walking in a rough way. It was like a dream, but it was a real experience. I encountered a bend in the road.

My plan to go to my workplace and to do things as usual did not work. I failed to realize that my plan was on my own terms and was what I wanted it to be. We may plan whatever we want to do today, but the Great Planner of life has said this, "My plans aren't your plans, nor are your ways my ways, says the LORD. Just as the heavens are higher than the earth, so are my ways higher than your ways, and my plans than your plans (Isa 55:8-10 CEB)." God's plans and paths are not the same as ordinary human plans. It does not matter how perfectly we organize life to execute plans, someone is around to divert our plans for the better plan that is according to his will.

Joseph planned to visit his brothers who were tending the flocks in the field. Before he got there, though, his brothers saw him coming and made a plan to kill him. Joseph ended up in the pit because of the wicked plan of his brothers. Daniel never expected to be thrown into a den of lions, but he ended up surrounded by the wild animals, who were ready to tear him apart. Furthermore, Daniel's three friends, Shadrach, Meshach, and Abednego, never thought that they would be in a fiery furnace. But because they refused to eat the food of King Nebuchadnezzar, they ended up in the deadly fire. All of these men's plans were struck down and crushed. However, the men came out safe!

Pain and trials never came to your mind either. You did not want pain and trials, but someone allows you to experience these once, twice, or more times during your life. I went through a seriously painful trial. I do not know why, and you do not know why you went through yours. We wish that we could have avoided it.

The Storm Hits Suddenly

Have you ever heard someone say, "Everything is going well?" While everything may be going well, suddenly something may happen very quickly and unpredictably. By the way, when you hear people say, "Life is unpredictable," this does not mean that they are negative people. It is true that we must walk by faith and not by sight (2 Cor 5:7). However, it is also true that real storms are out there. Life is surrounded by storms, and the storms never ask our permission to come to our places. A storm may come suddenly and hit everything in its way without warning, and no one can stop it.

The government may set up an excellent economic team chosen from the best universities to stop poverty. The government may recruit an expert in law enforcement and security to maintain the security of the nation. A meteorologist may predict the weather to alert people of future weather conditions. However, who can stop a severe storm when a powerful hurricane suddenly hits the southeastern part of the USA, causing enormous destruction and significant loss of life? Who can stop a sudden earthquake and tsunami that has afflicted people many times? Who could stop the evil minds of radical Muslims who suddenly blew up the World Trade Center and the Pentagon, leaving thousands of people dead? Who can prevent death when the doctor says that the cancer patient will die within three days? The answer is no one, and not even the experts.

I was about to finish writing this book and ready to send it to my publisher when suddenly the world was shaken by a deadly virus called "Coronavirus Disease (COVID-19)" killing a hundreds of thousands of people and infecting millions of people all over the world including me, my wife, and two of my sons. We followed the health guidance or protocols such as wearing a mask, washing hands with soap for at least 20 seconds, avoiding close contact with infected people, social distancing, etc. However, eight months after the coronavirus outbreak, the medical experts and scientists still cannot stop this contagious disease from spreading. How the pandemic presents in our lives, no one knows. We only hope and pray that the scientists and medical experts will soon find a solution to prevent the rampant spread of the pandemic and avoid more casualties.

David Jeremiah says that life is difficult. "Somewhere along your own path, you've likely encountered a bend in the road, too. Suddenly you faced circumstances you never expected or wished to encounter.[4]" Citing Gordon MacDonald, David Jeremiah goes on to say that God uses many tools "to bring blessing into the lives of His servants."[5]Gordon MacDonald calls one of the tools "disruptive moments," which are "those unanticipated events, most of which one would usually have chosen to avoid had it been possible."[6]These disruptive moments "are too often associated with pain and inconvenience, failure and humiliation."[7] No matter what precautions we take, no amount of preparation is adequate to prevent disruptive moments.

When I boarded the airplane and headed to my workplace, the captain announced from the cockpit that the weather was clear, the temperature was good, and we would be arriving on time. During the airborne time, nothing seemed out of the ordinary, except that we experienced some turbulence. However, a few minutes before landing, something went wrong. The airplane was shaking in the air. My heart started to race. All the passengers were in a panic. Some were screaming, some were praying, and all were waiting with an eerie feeling. Suddenly the airplane fell to ground, crashed into a rice field, and totally burned to ashes, which caused many deaths, as well as such severe injuries as burns and broken bones—including mine. My family found me in the hospital dying. All my plans on that day were ended. What was supposed to be a normal routine day became an abnormal, ruined day.

Each day, we spend time thinking and planning about the future and what lies ahead of us. We spend time thinking about the future and trying to anticipate what is around the corner, not realizing that a storm is also around the corner ready to hit in its own timing. Of course, some people who call themselves experts, prophets, or fortune tellers claim that they can see and predict the future accurately—but to no avail. They may think that trouble is miles away and that they are able to enjoy their golden day. However, suddenly they may face circumstances that they never expected on that day.

One day my family and I were sitting on the beautiful beach of Hawaii enjoying the sunshine and the gorgeous calm of the waves. Suddenly, a large wave came and swept away all the sand that we were sitting on, disrupting this beautiful panoramic view. We were all wet and had to move to higher ground. But suddenly several surfers came and ran into the sea in order to catch the big wave and to ride through the wave happily. For those of us who were sitting and lying down on the sand, the huge wave was a disruptive moment, but for the surfers, that same huge wave was a happy moment.

As long as the water fills the ocean, the ocean never stops producing waves. Either small or big, waves always come in their own time and way. The wave will sweep away everything in its path. The wave does not choose whose lives are impacted badly or beneficially. All of us who were sitting on the dry beach and the surfers on the beach were swept by the big wave. However, the surfers handled the wave well, took the benefit of the big wave, and it brought happiness to them—but we reacted differently. The sudden huge wave was a disruptive time for us, because it destroyed the dry sand on which we were sitting, and it brought us discomfort. The effects of the wave gave different impressions to us. I wish that I could have had a positive perception of the sudden raging wave, like the surfers, but I could not, because I did not know how to handle the wave like the surfers did.

I was sitting on the airplane comfortably, enjoying my flight on that day, but suddenly, the aircraft was shaking violently and crashed into the rice field. My comfort turned into a moment of distress, affliction, and pain. Like the surfers who were experts in handling a big wave, I wish that the pilot, who was trained well, could have controlled the aircraft to keep it from crashing. I wish that I could have enjoyed my flight, but I did not. Even so-called trained pilots cannot always deal with a sudden raging storm. The storm hit the plane so badly that it crashed to the ground and caused a horrible disaster, leaving pain and suffering for many people including me.

Be Careful of Comfort Zones

Where are you now? Are you enjoying your life? If that is your case, then I guess that you are in your comfort zone. I am referring to a "comfort zone" as being in a place of stability, security, and blessings. You do not want to leave the blessed moments of life. Thank God for the blessings. Enjoy your life with thanksgiving, because you deserve it. God loves to see His children have blessed lives. What does it mean to have a blessed life, anyway? Usually we relate this to success, wealth, job, health, or a family vacation to Hawaii, like mine. In other words, the common understanding of what it means to have a blessed life is that God gives us good things, and not bad things, such as disease, hardship, tribulation, etc. We want to be in a blessed life on our terms, all the days of our lives, because this is so comfortable.

Nobody wants to go through hardship, tribulation, pain, and suffering. We want to enjoy a season of God's security as our comfort zone. However, beware of complacency. The more you are on top and feeling secure, the closer you may be to falling. This does not mean that you do not trust God as you should, or because God has condemned you; rather, it is because God is a sovereign God. He gives and He takes away (Job 1:21). God is not a respecter of persons, and He does not show favoritism. There will be glory and honor and peace from God for all who do good, but also there will be trouble and calamity on this earth.

It is a false perception to say that wealth and health are designed for Christians, while poverty and disease are only intended for non-Christians. Wealth and health are not monopolized by Christians. Pain, suffering, and misery are not only for unbelievers—believers will also go through these. Whoever lives under the sun will experience good things or bad things, joy or sorrow (Ecclesiastes). The Father, who is in the heavens, causes His sun to rise on the evil and the good, and He sends rain on the just and unjust (Matt 5:45). In this respect, we can say that God's blessing is on everyone, believers and unbelievers alike. Likewise, pain and trouble are for everyone, believers and unbelievers.

I was sitting in seat 11 of that Boeing 737, enjoying my flight. However, when my plane went down that day, we all went down with it. All of us—whether in economy class or first class—were terrified in the horrific accident. According to the news, mostly passengers in the more comfortable first class were doomed, because the front end of the plane crashed on a hill before it landed in the rice paddy. Comfort and luxury do not guarantee security. It did not matter whether we flew first class or economy class—we were all in trouble that day. Jesus reminds us of this, "I have told you these things, so that in me you may have peace. In this world you will have trouble. But take heart! I have overcome the world (John 16:33)."

Feeling secure and comfortable in your life is okay; however, be sensitive to what comes next so that you can be as ready as possible for whatever might come your way. If you stay in your comfort zone and refuse to face the next wave of life, then you will never leave nor surpass your current reality. I wish for you to get run over by reality. However, waves are not intended to be calmed in all seasons. It all depends on the weather, and the weather is unpredictable. A ship is safe in a harbor, but that is not what a ship was built for. A ship was designed for sailing, ready to be out in the blowing winds and to stand against the waves.

I was enjoying my security and complacency for quite some time when God gave me an opportunity to build my career that I loved so dearly. My wife and I also had a good time raising our children and were happily building our family. We all enjoy a good life while we can. However, when hard times strike, then realize that both the good and the difficult come from God. Remember that nothing is certain in this life (Ecc 7:14). Solomon was explaining that when times are good, be happy, but when times are bad, be ready. Solomon, a king, a rich man, and full of wisdom, realized that there are seasons in life:

> To every *thing there* is a season, and a time to every purpose under the heaven; a time to be born, and a time to die; a time to plant, and a time to pluck up *that which is* planted; a time to kill, and a time to heal; a time to break down, and a time to build up; a time to weep,

and a time to laugh; a time to mourn, and a time to dance; a time to cast away stones, and a time to gather stones together; a time to embrace, and a time to refrain from embracing; a time to get, and a time to lose; a time to keep, and a time to cast away; a time to rend, and a time to sew; a time to keep silence, and a time to speak; a time to love, and a time to hate; a time of war, and a time of peace. (Ecc 3:1-8 KJV)

God has an eternal plan for everyone, and that includes all the intentions and activities of everyone on earth. We can do whatever we want to do in this earth. God gives us a free will. We can choose to stay in our comfort zones, or exit from them, but God knows all the intentions of our hearts. He knows whether our complacency will make us better or not. Additionally, if our current convenience will not make us better, then God will disrupt our comfort and change the times and seasons to redirect our plans and paths, even if this hurts us, just to make us to become better persons for His own purposes.

When God asked Jonah to go to Nineveh to preach, he refused to go and went toward Tarshish instead. Jonah chose to travel to Tarshish by ship, where he thought he could find a perfect place for his comfort zone. As a result, Jonah was in trouble. The reason why Jonah was in trouble was because he did not want to align with the heart of God for his call. Jonah felt uncomfortable going to Nineveh, because he did not like the people of Nineveh. But God has a loving heart, even for Nineveh. Jonah did not want to make a commitment when he felt comfortable. God had to shake up Jonah's comfortable world. In his disobedience to God, Jonah had to pay an expensive price for running from God. Jonah was thrown from the ship that he was on into the sea, and God allowed a big fish to swallow him for three days.

Jonah was in big trouble. God used the fish to disrupt Jonah's comfort zone. God utilized the suffering and trouble of the recalcitrant prophet to redirect his way back to Nineveh in order to better his own life and to bless the people of Nineveh. God prepared a more valuable life for Jonah, but first, Jonah had to get out of his comfort zone and experience pain. God gave Jonah a wake-up call for his better use. God shook Jonah's comfort zone and moved him out from it for his greater life breakthrough. Jonah admitted that God turned his comfort zone into discomfort, but Jonah used it as point of return to God. From discomfort and trouble, Jonah cried out to God from inside the fish:

> In my distress I called to the LORD, and he answered me. From deep in the realm of the dead I called for help, and you listened to my cry. You hurled me into the depths, into the very heart of the seas, and the currents swirled about me; all your waves and breakers swept over me. I said, "I have been banished from your sight; yet I will look again toward your holy temple." The engulfing

waters threatened me, the deep surrounded me; seaweed was wrapped around my head. To the roots of the mountains I sank down; the earth beneath barred me in forever. But you, LORD my God, brought my life up from the pit. (Jonah 2:2-6)

Jonah realized that he was disobedient, and he knew that it was God who threw him into the sea. However, when Jonah humbled his heart and was willing to step out from his comfort zone, God heard his prayer and saved his life from the pit. Jonah released his self-security to receive God's solemn duty prepared for him.

Chapter 2

PAIN AND SUFFERING ARE REAL

"I have told you these things, so that in me you may
have peace. In this world you will have trouble.
But take heart! I have overcome the world."
(John 16:33)

All of us would like to enjoy a smooth life without disturbing moments. We all dislike suffering. Therefore, we do not like to hear what we dislike. For that reason, it is rare to hear preachers preach a theology of suffering today, because suffering and pain can bring people down. and some preachers do not want to make people feel stressed and disappointed. The preacher may say, "Congregations do not want to hear a message of suffering and tribulation anymore; they have enough pain and heartache."

Some preachers may be trying to make their congregations happy in order to keep them in their churches. These preachers may want to entertain people by assuring them that by being believers, they will not experience trials and tribulation, but only joy and laughter. These pastors want to preach the theology of prosperity to let the congregants know that being a Christian is all about abundance and prosperity. These pastors become preachers of the prosperity Gospel and the entertainment Gospel and are not the revealers of the whole truth of the Scripture. Therefore, when tribulation happens, congregants may find themselves wavering and even running from God, instead of running to God. Congregants are frantically searching for prosperity and enjoyment that they believe is the Christian life, rather than living faithfully in God. Mere prosperity will not teach congregants to bear the weight of their burdens. Without a theology of suffering, congregants will assume that something is wrong and out of balance. They become very vulnerable when pain and trials strike. These congregants will come to the conclusion that suffering is an abnormal state, or even a punishment from God.

The Bible recounts many testings and trials, both in the Old and New Testaments. For example, the book of Exodus tells of the Israelites' forty years of being in the wilderness. The book of Job narrates the account of the most suffering man ever in his time. The book of Psalms describes the anguish of David and other writers. The four Gospels depict the sufferings of Jesus Christ, the central figure of the Scripture itself. The Bible narrates both pain and pleasure, sorrow and joy, poverty and prosperity.

Of course, God is a God of abundance and prosperity, and it is His will to make us prosper. God promised it. The Scriptures declare it: "But remember the LORD your God, for it is he who gives you the ability to produce wealth, and so confirms his covenant, which he swore to your ancestors, as it is today (Deut 8:18)." God blessed Israel as a sign or endorsement that He was fulfilling His covenant with Abraham and his descendants. In the same book, God repeated His promise: "Then the LORD your God will make you most prosperous in all the work of your hands and in the fruit of your womb, the young of your livestock and the crops of your land. The LORD will again delight in you and make you prosperous, just as he delighted in your fathers (Deut 30:9)."

God said that whatever they touched, let it be turned to blessing. God wanted to make Israel wealthy through the work of their hands. God is pleased to see us prosper in every area of our lives. The prosperity promises were not only given to the people of Israel, but to all the believers, including you and me. It is a desire of God to see us blessed in every area of life, not only in wealth but also in health, as John says: "Beloved, I pray that in every way you may succeed *and* prosper and be in good health [physically], just as [I know] your soul prospers [spiritually] (3 John 2 AMP)."

You see, God not only wants to make us wealthy materially, but also healthy physically and spiritually, and that is abundance in prosperity. However, God blesses us not simply so that we can brag about it. Or God gives us healthy bodies not simply so that we can feel good. God does these things for us, for His name's sake. The reason for God to prosper us by giving us blessed and healthy lives is His commitment to His own glory. God acts in His own way to protect His glory. God deserves all the glory. When God promises to prosper us, He will do it because He will not and cannot break His own promise. Solomon admits that he was blessed because God made His promise to his father David, and God kept it. "You have kept your promise to your servant David my father; with your mouth you have promised and with your hand you have fulfilled it (2 Chr 6:15)."

Likewise, when we have pain today, God allows it so that His name will be glorified in it. He allows this to happen to protect His reputation—and His reputation is at stake in it. God does not want the devil to rejoice over your pain. Therefore, God's promise is to heal you, and He has the strength to back it up. Keeping His promise brings glory to God. Therefore, if you are not living with wealth materially and health physically at this moment, it does not mean that God does not love you or that you do not have faith. Or when you are at a low ebb spiritually, it does not mean that God has abandoned you.

David the psalmist experienced such moments as he expressed in Psalm 22. Almost the whole chapter describes David's anguish. He is expressing his feelings while being abandoned by God, while being in dreadful pain and surrounded by enemies, and while suffering and be treated unfairly by God. David expressed his moment of pain in a most grieved and anguished statement: "My God, my God, why have you forsaken me? (Ps 22:1)." This is the same expression made by Jesus during His suffering on the cross: "About three in the afternoon Jesus cried out in a loud voice, '*Eli, Eli, lema sabachthani?*' (which means 'My God, my God, why have you forsaken me?') (Matt 27:46)." In an anguished loud voice, Jesus expressed His pain and suffering.

In the midst of His suffering in the garden of Gethsemane, Jesus prayed, "Father, if you are willing, take this cup from me; yet not my will, but yours be done (Luke 22:42)." Indeed, Jesus' suffering was the will of His Father. Jesus' suffering had to end up in His death on Calvary to take our place, so that our pain and suffering would not cause our death but would help us have victorious and abundant life in Him.

You see, Jesus Himself, our Savior, went through trials, but many times we just want Jesus to suffer alone. We just want His gain, but not His pain. We want to give a nice testimony but are not willing to accept a heartache testing. There is no testimony without testing. A blessed testimony must be proven by a real testing, otherwise it is a false testimony. It is good to say that "God is good all the time and all the time God is good." However, it is wrong to say, "If you become a Christian, life is always good." This is a misleading testimony.

David Jeremiah, a renown pastor, teacher, and cancer survivor expresses, "There is a strange idea going around in churches today. Some Christians have the odd impression that being a believer will exempt them from all problems. Somehow, they feel that, upon conversion, they're issued the spiritual equivalent of ID cards that say, 'This absolves the holder from any kind of pain or trouble while living on this planet.'"[1]

When Paul says in Romans 8:28, "And we know that in all things God works for the good of those who love him, who have been called according to his purpose," he does not mean that life is always good. However, in all things—joy and sorrow; mourning and dancing; blessing and pain; pleasure and affliction—God can make/use all these things for our own good. What is good for us does not necessarily mean that it is good for God. However, what is good for God is good for us. God knows us far better than we know ourselves (Rom 8:27). We must understand that there is gain through pain. God knows that everything that we experience in life, good or bad, eventually will work for our own good. Although we do not understand it at the time when the pain strikes, ultimately, we will understand it.

Be Realistic

God never promised a fairy-tale life for people. Have you seen someone who never experiences pain? Or can you find a person who never, or never will, go through pain and suffering due to denying it? If you cannot find one, then allow me to agree with you that pain and suffering are unavoidable, and they are parts of life. Peter warns us that we must not be indifferent toward trials: "My dear friends, do not be surprised at the painful test you are suffering, as though something unusual were happening to you" (1 Pet 4:12 GNT). Peter reminds us that pain and suffering are not some strange things but are parts of life. We cannot reject them nor deny them. They may hit us suddenly without our permission, because they are parts of life. As long as we live in this temporary world, we will face pain and suffering. The Bible relates many painful narratives about people before they experienced healing. People who were in pain unashamedly cried out loud to God asking for help. Listen to the cry of David when he said, "In my distress I called to the LORD; I cried to my God for help (Ps 18:6)."

We should not be surprised by this, but rather we should prepare for it by following the example of Jesus. This was why David was so realistic about trials and tribulations. David declared that the Lord was his Shepherd (Ps 23). God is a good Shepherd who provided David graciously with a superabundance of food and water. God was David's provider, and he did not lack. David also declared that the good Shepherd was his protector. David was proclaiming his confidence in the One who blessed him abundantly and who protected him from the snares of enemies. David was talking about prosperity in every aspect of life. Prosperity is more than money or health. It is *shalom* in Hebrew.

According to the Brown-Driver-Briggs *Hebrew and English Lexicon of the Old Testament, shalom* is "completeness, soundness, welfare, peace," and includes wholeness and "prosperity."[2] In Psalm 23, David was resting in safety, assured that he would experience the favor of God, completeness and protection, and that he would lack nothing. David even assured that when you walk through the fire, you will not be burned; the flames will not set you ablaze (Ps 43:2). However, David was very realistic in what he said.

Along with this assurance, there was a valley and a wilderness around him. David warned that there are trials, afflictions, pain, and suffering, because assurance does not mean being free from the wilderness.

Through his Shepherd's Psalm, David reminds us that assurance will not free us from pain. Assurance gives you confidence that God will pick you up when you are down, but it does not mean that you are never down. Assurance gives you encouragement that God will fill you with His presence when you feel lonely, but it does not mean that you are never lonely. Assurance means that when you cry, God will wipe all your tears, but it does not mean that you will never cry. Assurance gives the promise that God will be your comforter when you feel sad, but it does not mean that you are never sad. Why? Because God has His own agenda for every one of us, the sheep of His flock, and we never know His agenda because He is a sovereign God. At the same time, we must realize that God will never place us in a situation that we cannot handle. God knows what He is doing. Paul assures us that God is a faithful God, and "He will not let you be tempted beyond what you can bear. But when you are tempted, he will also provide a way out so that you can endure it (1 Cor 10:13)."

David knew that he was on the mountain top of blessing that day, but he also realized that one day he might be in the darkest valley of death. David was very aware of the gravity of the world. Having seen what David went through, I guess, Solomon was inspired to echo the unpredictable nature of the wilderness of his father by saying, "Do not boast about tomorrow, for you do not know what a day may bring (Prov 27:1)." You may be very healthy and strong today, or you may be wealthy today with big savings and a nice insurance package to assure that your future is safe. However, do not rely on these. Put your trust in God. He knows what tomorrow holds. I know that your flesh does not want to experience the gravities of the world: pain and suffering, trials and afflictions. You want to enjoy a stable life and comfortable moments. Nevertheless, friends, always buckle up—who knows what turbulence ahead of you could suddenly shake your world.

As mentioned, I was sitting relaxed in the aircraft, enjoying my flight, and thinking about my routine meeting with my staff as soon as I got to my office. Not long after, the pilot announced that in a minute we would be landing. Suddenly, a moment of relaxation turned into a moment of panic, and a moment of panic turned into many stressful moments, and those stressful moments turned into a doomed day as the aircraft crashed into the ground. Ah, David was so right. His experience was so real. I was just enjoying a moment of relaxation in the air, but suddenly I was experiencing a moment of despair in the darkest valley of death. I went through a near-death experience. The gravity of the world suddenly sucked my aircraft down to the ground. I do not know why it happened. I did not even know which hospital I was taken to. The only thing that I knew was that the magnitude of my pain and suffering took many months to resolve, moving from one hospital to another hospital, afflicted with severe burns, injuries, and a broken shoulder. I was in the hospital, battling between life and death, and I went through the darkest time of my life.

May you never experience a horrific event like mine. Perhaps this is the happiest moment for you, friends. You can laugh and enjoy your moments. However, if you have such a moment as you are reading this book, then do not worry, because it will not last long. There is a time for everything. Everything that happens in this world happens at the time that God chooses (Prov 3:1).

Pain and Suffering Will Not Last Long

Peter told us that pain and suffering are part of life, but God is healing through the process, even if we do not realize it. Peter assures us that following suffering, joy will come exceedingly: "But rejoice inasmuch as ye are partakers of Christ's sufferings; that, when his glory shall be revealed, ye may be glad also with exceeding joy" (1 Pet 4:12-13 KJV).

When you read how David described his affliction in Psalm 22, you may feel aching and stuck, knowing the horrible impact of afflictions in life. But hold on—in a moment, after going through all his afflictions and trials, David made a bold declaration in Psalm 23. Psalm 22 shows just how tough and ruthlessly honest David could be. It tells us about a tremendous suffering with no relief from God. David was helpless and exhausted. All he could do was cry to God. However, in Psalm 23, David opens with a very convincing declaration saying, "The LORD is my shepherd; I shall not want (NKJV)."

What a profound statement made by David shortly after his pain. David closes with a profession of absolute confidence in God. God leads children lovingly through life, and He cares for them as His flock. The Shepherd's Psalm is probably the best known and the best loved of all the psalms. Psalm 23 captures the essence of David's confidence in God. After his desperate situation, somehow David manages to make God the center of his life and to trust in Him fully, declaring that God is his provider and protector.

The outcome of David's experience in his pain was so comforting and encouraging to us. Right after his desperate situation, David gained greater confidence in God. After David's dark time, God's bright light shines. It will not be too long before your dark time will be turning to light. David had left a legacy: victory through suffering.

In another of his psalms, David showed more confidence by repeating the narrative about the sparkling of a new season after the old season. David was confident that his weeping would turn into shouts of joy. Psalm 30:5 says, "For his anger lasts only a moment, but his favor lasts a lifetime; weeping may stay for the night but rejoicing comes in the morning." It is a promise that will come to pass. The joy will prevail over sorrow. Therefore, David was thanking God for *dark nights* and for *joyful mornings*.

In the same psalm, David wrote a beautiful poem declaring that God is more than able to change his situation no matter what. In Psalm 30:11, David wrote, "You have changed my sadness into a joyful dance; you have taken away my sorrow and surrounded me with joy (GNT)." David is probably the most helpful example concerning pain and suffering in the Old Testament. His psalms provide abundant teaching on hardship through his life's examples. In his exposition of Psalm 30, C. H. Spurgeon explains:

> Throughout this Psalm there are indications that David had been greatly afflicted, both personally and relatively, after having, in his presumption, fancied himself secure. When God's children prosper one way, they are generally tried another, for few of us can bear unmingled prosperity. Even the joys of hope need to be mixed with the pains of experience, and the more surely so when comfort breeds carnal security and self-confidence. Nevertheless, pardon soon followed repentance, and God's mercy was glorified.[3]

Truly, God never changes, but He can change our situation when we keep holding on to Him. Such desperate events were also experienced by Joseph. He had to go through the pit and prison before he ended up in the palace. Nevertheless, Joseph still could pray in his persecution and praise in his prison. Therefore, God brought Joseph into the palace to enjoy paradise. The same type of life events happened to Daniel. Daniel was in exile. He was put into the foreign king's training and into an education program with simple food, then he was put into a lion's den before God elevated him to a position of far-reaching impact and influence. In all these events, though, Daniel remained faithful to God. Our willingness to wait and to remain faithful before God is a key to opening a new season. God is never surprised by our pain and suffering. He knows what we are going through and will help us pass through it. Pain and suffering; however, will not last forever.

Waiting Patiently

Waiting for the recovery of health is not an easy thing. Waiting can be frustrating. We all know it. I have been there, and maybe some of you have, too. After staying in the hospital for six months, my wife nursed me for another eight months at home before I fully recovered. Waiting for the healing process of burned skin was a real heartache. Many times, when my wife was cleaning and dressing my wounds, her eyes filled with tears. She witnessed unending dry wounds and the changing color of wounds. Today my wounds might be a red color, tomorrow they could turn to black, and another day they could turn to purple. Today my wound would be dry, but tomorrow it could become raw again. The doctor said that it was impossible for the skin to heal at once—it would heal layer by layer. Skin has three layers: the epidermis (the outermost layer of skin), the dermis (beneath the epidermis), and the hypodermis (the deeper subcutaneous tissue). No wonder my healing process was so slow.

After enduring skin grafts several times, my skin fully recovered from the burn wounds. However, it never returned to normal, and the doctor had said that it would not. Furthermore, the battle with skin keloids was another frustrating thing. A keloid is a raised scar after the skin has healed that can grow to be much larger than the original injury. Sleeping face down, which I never did before, was another hardship. The doctor suggested this to speed up the healing of a severe burn wound on my back. I slept face down for months. Frustration, worry, and anger mixed together. It is too hard to explain at that moment.

In my frustration, I kept asking, "God, what's wrong with me? Why me? Why should I go through this?" Anyone who has gone through pain knows how hard it is to remain silent when the pressure comes. In my confusion and despair, though, God did not leave me alone. His grace was enough for me. He gave me the ability to endure the pain and hardship. He gave me the ability to say, "It is well with my soul."

The hymn was written by Horatio G. Spafford after he had gone through many afflictions. His son died, then the Great Chicago Fire struck, which was financially disastrous. To make it worse, the tragedy struck again. His wife and four daughters were on a ship that sank in the dark waters of the Atlantic Ocean on their way to England. "More than two hundred lives were lost, including the Spafford's' four daughters." In that tragedy, "Mrs. Spafford cabled her husband with the words 'saved alone.'" Following all these tragedies, Mr. Spafford penned his hymn.[5]

After six months in hospitals, and another eight months of waiting for recovery at home, you probably ask: did I feel aggrieved about my pain and complain about what I had gone through for such long time? Honestly, yes, I did. I felt worn out and frustrated. I was impatient, and I complained about the things that I did not understand. I used to be active, but suddenly I was locked down and crippled. I was questioning God about what was going wrong with me, as well as why it took so long to recover. But this did not last long, and I did not allow myself to be dominated by complaints, because complaining would not give me any help. God gave me a feeling of peace, and He reminded me again of what He said to me in my previous dream, that I should not hold on to my "why" questions, and I should quit feeling like I needed to know everything. In waiting, I also learned how to trust God for His time, instead of focusing on "when" questions. I decided not to try to figure out when I would be recovered. Rather, I made up my mind that I would not give up until I was fully recovered.

Whether we are believers or non-believers, we still go through trials and hardships if we live out a normal life length. No one is immune to these. Life with God is not immunity to pain and suffering. David Jeremiah adds, "We Christians have no immunity whatsoever to pain or suffering. It matters not whether you're a new convert or a wise spiritual giant, you're still an imperfect human creature living in a fallen world; you struggle with all the blessings and burdens being a member of the family of man entails."[6] If this is the reality of life, then we had better wait patiently, rather than complaining and being frustrated. It will not last long, for the new season always will come.

The Scripture does not tell how long David had to wait for his situation to change, but I find that the secret to David's endurance was his desire to give praise to God in the midst of his painful situations. In Psalm 30:12, David says "that my heart may sing your praises and not be silent. LORD my God, I will praise you forever." All people who trust while waiting have proven that the goodness of God will be displayed. Running from difficult situations only adds more pain, but waiting on God's way can produce patience, and patience can develop during time of afflictions and hardships. James encourages us to "let patience have *its* perfect work, that you may be perfect and complete, lacking nothing" (Jas 1:4 NKJV). Isaiah also reminds us of the benefit of waiting, when he beautifully wrote, "But they that wait upon the LORD shall renew *their* strength; they shall mount up with wings as eagles; they shall run, and not be weary; *and* they shall walk, and not faint (Isa 40:31, KJV)."

This is the reason why I say, "Pain and suffering will not last long." God gave us an ability to wait patiently, rather than complain, because complaining will distract us and rob us of our joy while we are waiting. Ask for God's counsel for every step of your healing journey. Do not mask your pain. This will only make it difficult to heal. God knows how to heal what is broken and how to restore what is missing.

Consider the following person: Marcella was trying to fill what was missing in her life. Marcella was married to a man who was raised in church and who believed there was a

God, but who did not live for Christ. She and her husband lived a worldly life, using a wide variety of drugs, including marijuana, quaaludes, hash, THC, opium, speed, and alcohol. Marcella searched through every evil thing, including drugs, alcohol, worldly music, and promiscuity. She had two sons, but she ended up divorcing her husband due to his alcohol abuse. Later, though, they remarried for many reasons. And they started a new life. They attended church regularly and read the Bible regularly. Unfortunately, they gradually started missing church and stopped reading the Bible as often as they had. An acquaintance introduced her husband to narcotics, and slowly but surely, he got drawn into the world of cocaine. Marcella's husband spent his entire paycheck on cocaine, and he was gone for days at a time. More and more frequently, they stayed home from church, and finally they stopped going altogether. She tried to find what was missing to fill the emptiness, but nothing helped—until she came back to God and followed His leading. She began praying and serving God and she was blessed to see her oldest son become a pastor. Marcella realized what it means to wait patiently until God brought her and her family into amazing healing. In her true story, Marcella admits that Jesus left the ninety-nine and came back to rescue her.[7]

In my waiting for recovery, I even had an opportunity to write my book—lying face down—called *Escape from Death*, to encourage people to have faith in God while in times of despair. In waiting patiently, you allow God's presence to invade your heart. In waiting on God, you allow Him to visit you. In waiting on God, you allow Him to abide in you, and you in Him. The Scripture says, "If you abide in Me, and My words abide in you, you will ask what you desire, and it shall be done for you. By this my Father is glorified, that you bear much fruit; so you will be My disciples (John 15:7-8 NKJV)." Asking for deliverance from hardship and trials relates to our obedience to wait and to abide in God. Isaiah gave the Lord's words to Israel, "If you repented and patiently waited for me, you would be delivered; if you calmly trusted in me you would find strength (Isa 30:15 NET)." This is the reason why the trials will not last too long, because in waiting, God gives strength and joy, and in joy, we gain patient hearts.

The time to wait to be delivered from hardship becomes insignificant to you if you are willing to wait upon the Lord. Joseph waited for thirteen years. He moved from place to place, from pit to prison, and from prison to palace. That was the best time to make him ready to enter his new season as second in command of all of Egypt. I pray that you are also ready to welcome your new season of life, patiently.

Chapter 3

LIFE IS FULL OF QUESTIONS

"No one can comprehend what goes on under the sun. Despite all their efforts to search it out, no one can discover its meaning. Even if the wise claim they know, they cannot really comprehend it."
(Ecclesiastes 8;17)

The Question of "Why Me?"

Conversation is the most important thing in human communication. Conversation connects us to people and to God. In conversation, we express ourselves in many ways. One of many ways to express ourselves is to ask a question. A question helps us find a way—it even helps us find God. A question is used to get information on something that we do not understand, since life sometimes can throw us pain that is too much to handle. A question helps us understand the situation, which often makes us wonder: why did this happen to me?

In my desperate situation, in the aftermath of the airplane crash, I did question God about what had befallen me. I was asking an open-ended question, using my own feelings to try to get an explanation from God. I asked God, "Why did this tragedy happen to me?" When God afflicts us, it is desirable to know the reason, regardless of the answer. We would rather question God, be it right or wrong, than accept the mystery of the pain and suffering. Our instinct wants to investigate what went wrong with us. Timothy Keller writes, "When suffering first hits you, the gap between what you know with the mind and what you can use out of your store of knowledge in your heart can be surprisingly large. When troubles come, you will need God's help to find the particular insight, consoling thoughts, and wisdom you will need to get through."[1] All the thoughts are articulated in the form of questions.

Some believe that questioning God Himself is a sign of disbelief or heresy. I believe that asking God "why" does not make us bad persons. God knows that we have a desire to ask about things that we do not understand. I believe that questioning God with a humble heart to get the wisdom of God—rather than questioning God's authority to validate our ways—would be a proper conversation with God.

Many people, including people recorded in the Scriptures, went through hardships and asked "why" questions. Moses questioned God's motives for calling Moses to lead the Israelites out of Egypt. Gideon questioned God concerning why the Midianites ravaged the crops and the livestock, leaving the countryside totally impoverished.

In this desperate situation, the Israelites had been severely oppressed. In the midst of this situation, Gideon, a prophet of Israel, was suddenly greeted by an angel. However, before the angel was able to instruct Gideon in the way of the Lord, Gideon interrupted with several questions. "'But sir,' Gideon replied, 'If the Lord is with us, why has all this happened to us? Where are all his wonders that our fathers told us about when they said, "Did not the Lord bring us up out of Egypt? But now the Lord has abandoned us and put us into the hand of Midian' (Judg 6:13-14)." Gideon questioned God about why the Israelites had been severely oppressed by the Midianites for seven years consecutively. However, we learn that God never answers Gideon's "why" questions directly. Instead, the only thing that God wanted from Gideon was to be obedient in being appointed to save Israel from the Midianites.

When I went through devastating moments right after I regained consciousness from the airplane crash, I bombarded God with a barrage of questions concerning why this tragedy happened to me. I demanded an instant answer. Sadly, God did not answer me, even when I toned it down with a humble heart. When tribulations attack, then the most common reaction of human beings to the tragedy is to question God with one simple question: "Why?" They think that God might give them an answer. Unfortunately, God is not obligated to answer our questions. This does not mean that God does not listen to our cries, but it does mean that His ways are not our ways, and His plan is not our plan—and surely God has His unique plans for us. God does not bind Himself to our will concerning how He operates. He is only bound to Himself. His choices do not depend on our personal wills.

Jesus did not come into the world to stop suffering nor to explain it so that we can understand and figure it out; rather, Jesus promised to be around when suffering hits us. I knew this, but I asked Him anyway because I was desperate for the answer. God is a sovereign God; He has His own ways and plans. However, the "why" questions are the most common questions raised when people go through pain and suffering.

A poll was taken by the Ventura, California, based Barna Group. In the poll, the question was asked, "If you could ask God one question and you knew He would give you an answer, what would you ask?" The most common response was, "Why is there pain and suffering in the world?"[2] When the storm hits, it will not be long until you will hear some people question God and blame God for it. The most common practice is using an open-ended question that demands an explanation to satisfy their grudging feelings. People will ask, "How could a God of love allow tragedy, pain, and suffering? If God exists, then why does He allow suffering, disaster, or calamity?" Sometimes people will ask a seemingly self-defending question, "If I love God, why is life so hard; why doesn't God make life easy? Why do we have many problems?"

Greg Laurie wrote that "C. S. Lewis said, 'The problem of pain is atheism's most potent weapon against the Christian faith.' Most people point to the problem of evil and suffering as their reason for not believing in God than any other. . . .

So, why does God allow tragedy? If God can prevent such terrible tragedies, why does He allow them to take place?" Their classic statement about this problem is: "Either God is all powerful but not all good, and therefore He doesn't stop evil—or He's all good but not all powerful, and therefore He can't stop evil."[3]

For them, the goodness of God has nothing to do with pain; pain is the work of evil. Therefore, when bad things happen to human beings, God is to be blamed for it, because He allowed bad things to happen and did not protect people from evil. Timothy Keller says, "In the secular view, suffering is never seen as a meaningful part of life but only as an interruption. With that understanding, there are only two things to do when pain and suffering occur. The first is to manage and lessen the pain. . . . The second way to handle suffering in this framework is to look for the cause of the pain and eliminate it."[4]

People who do not want to accept the reality of pain and suffering have set their own criteria about the goodness of God. They make their set standards for goodness equal to the goodness of God. For them, goodness is to live happily and prosperously. These people say that when something is good for them, then it should also good for God. They say that God's greatest desire should be their happiness. Therefore, happiness and the prosperity message have become the principal theologies of their lives. They do not realize that God's goodness does not depend on their feelings. God is still good, whether they feel happy or not. The goodness of God is not determined or defined by conditions. God is good because

He has said that He is! Jesus said, "No one is good—except God alone" (Luke 18:19).

God is a good God even when He has not answered, nor ever gives an answer to, our "why" questions on the tragedy that has befallen us. Many times, the "why" questions are not answered, not because God does not hear our cries nor care about us, but because He may have other plans for our own good and a better future. God will reveal the answer in His own way and time. Jeremiah assured us about this: "'For I know the plans I have for you,' declares the LORD, 'plans to prosper you and not to harm you, plans to give you hope and a future'" (Jer 29:11). The "why" questions are not answered, not because they were not appropriate questions, but because we may need some time for preparation to handle the answers. Or maybe God wanted us to change our questions.

Change Your "Why" Questions into "What" Questions

In our trials, we often ask God "why," believing that God will provide us with a satisfactory answer. The "why" questions come up in our minds because something happened to us beyond our comprehension. God does not forbid us from asking questions, because He is a good and compassionate God. He feels what we feel, because we are created in His image. He can feel our cries and sorrow, and He can feel our fear, and He can see our tears. How do I know this?

The Scripture has promised it. Isaiah announces God's word, "Fear not, for I *am* with you; be not dismayed, for I *am* your God; I will strengthen you, yes, I will help you, I will uphold you with My righteous right hand (Isa 41:10 NKJV)." God knows that we have fear—this is why He says, "Fear not." God knows that we become dismayed—this is why He comforts us. God knows that we are weak—this is why He strengthen us. God knows how many times we are helpless—this is why He helps and sustain us. The promises from this verse are the compassion of God for us: (1) to give the grace and strength needed to deal with all these life situations; (2) to help us through times of crises as the source of our security and welfare; and (3) to sustain us and defend us. I believe that some of you who have been going through the storms of life also have experienced these beautiful promises of God, and you will continue to receive them when you go through hardships as you hold on to Him.

Not long after the death of Moses, God asked Joshua to take Moses' place to lead Israel to the promised land. Joshua was nervous and discouraged. He knew that his leadership was nothing compared to Moses'. He knew the Israelites' behavior and how they treated Moses. Nevertheless, Joshua was encouraged by God, who said, "Be strong and coura-geous! Do not be terrified or dismayed (intimidated), for the LORD your God is with you wherever you go (Josh 1:9 AMP)." God gave Joshua strength and courage to lead His people. God's promise was fulfilled, and Joshua brought Israel into the land.

The promises are there for you. You may claim them. Claiming is not bad, as some people may think. It is a privilege of God's children to claim by faith, with humble hearts, and to let the will of God be done—because in the end, it is not because of our faith, but because of the faithfulness of God. We just read that Isaiah and Joshua received the promises of comfort, strength, and encouragement fulfilled by God even before they said anything. The Lord loves a humble heart. God is watching and waiting to favor His children. The Scripture says, "You do not have because you do not ask God (Jas 4:2)." God rejoices when we ask, because this indicates our dependency on Him. In fact, He is waiting for us to ask for His help. However, when we ask, it does not mean that we will always get what we ask for. James goes on saying, "When you ask, you do not receive, because you ask with wrong motives, that you may spend what you get on your pleasures" (Jas 4:3). God refuses to answer an ambitious prayer for self-pleasure and self-honor. All of us must pay attention, because God will not listen to our prayers if our hearts are full of selfish desires. Or God may have a better promise and purpose for us to fulfill and, therefore, our prayers have not been answered yet.

Likewise, when it comes to questioning our sorrow or brokenness, too often we do not get the answer that we want. It turns out that the "why" questions will not help. Laura Story (a worship leader and recording artist), when her husband Martin was diagnosed with a brain tumor, expressed her thoughts on this: "It's important to know that nowhere does the Bible promise that all our questions will be answered this side of heaven. God doesn't promise our stories will make sense in and of themselves. But he does promise they will find their greater purpose in light of his greater story of redemption."[5]

The lives of Laura and her husband were never the same. Yes, with God all things are possible. However, the devastating news was that no cure existed to restore her husband's short-term memory, eyesight, and other complications. The fairy-tale life that Laura had dreamed of was no longer possible. Nevertheless, in struggling with God about how to live with broken dreams, Laura found joy and a deeper intimacy with Jesus.

I surrendered to burn injuries, and I stayed in the hospital for six months. I could not even move myself. The first three months of my pain and suffering were the most devastating times. During the first two months, the doctor gave me twenty-two types of antibiotics to kill the bacteria in my burn wounds, but to no avail. In the third month, however, the doctor stated that my wound was infected by a strong bacterium called Pseudomonas and Methicillin Resistant Staphylococcus Aureus (MRSA). The doctor said that a strong bacterium like this must be killed with strong antibiotics. The problem, though, was that the hospital only had one more type of antibiotic that was very strong, and there was a possibility that my body would react badly to it. The prediction of the doctor came to pass. As the antibiotic was administered by infusion, I suddenly felt dizzy, my head felt heavy, and my skin began to swell and feel itchy. There was an adverse reaction. The nurse immediately stopped the infusion and rushed to contact the medical team. Spontaneously I cried out, "*Why has this happened to me? How much more of this can I take?*" In my desperate situation, I kept asking God the same question: "*Why?*" That was all that I could do. I felt so devastated, and I needed the answers to satisfy my injured feelings. Through tears, my wife and I were asking God, "Why?" In every stage of my pain and suffering, from the first day of the airplane crash, to my death's-door reaction to the failure of the last antibiotics that were supposed to save my life, the "why" questions kept coming to my mind. I was playing the blame game and focusing on my pain. I had a number of "why" questions to ask God. Unfortunately, God never answered my why question; rather, He asked me to forget my "why" questions, and He asked me to change them to "what" questions. God gave me a freedom, and I found joy in my heart and purpose in life as I put aside the "why" and begin to ask "what." The "why" questions only caused me to get stuck and caused me more pain, but the "what" questions allowed me to surrender, humbling to the will of God, and to do willingly whatever fit Him.

Understanding the Role of Questions in Pain

God has His own ways. He knows what has happened to us. He knows why it has happened. He can do whatever He wants, and He can design something for us in whatever He wants us to be. Of course, we have a free will to choose. Do you remember that Adam and Eve had the right to choose from every fruit in the garden but one, "the tree of the knowledge of good and evil (Gen 2:17)"—the one that was so sacred and honored to God? This only belonged to God. No one was supposed to mess with it. The result of messing with this tree's fruit was fatal. However, Adam and Eve messed with it anyway. You know the end of the story. Adam and Eve were banished from the beautiful garden that they were supposed to enjoy. As a result of their rebellious hearts, all of us understand how we got here and why there is so much pain, suffering, destruction, trials, and death in the world in which we live. Using free will to choose the desire of our hearts may be okay, but it is not okay to contest the will of God. God was not being too hard to not allow Adam and Eve to eat the fruit from the tree of the knowledge of good and evil, but God wanted to test their obedience. Indeed, "testing is necessary to build character and develop maturity."[6]

God will test us in a specific area to see if we will have the strength and character in our personalities to be able to override the desires of our egos and to be willing to obey God over all our wants and desires. I wanted to know "why" the pain happened to me that caused my family and me great suffering for almost one and a half years. I wanted to know "why" my airplane crashed, even though I prayed for a safe and peaceful flight before I flew that morning. I wanted to ask God "why," believing that the answers would provide me with deep soul satisfaction. Again, I did not get the answers that I wanted. One night, though, in a precious and appointed moment, God visited me and spoke to me the reasons "why" it all happened to me.

God spoke three reasons. The first and second reasons were truly satisfying, because they were a promise of healing, and I rejoiced in this. However, before God gave me the third reason, suddenly God asked me to change my "why" question to a "what" question. Gladly I changed my question: "Lord, what do you want me to do?" What a shocking answer I received—the answer that I did not want to hear. God asked me to leave my worldly career behind. This was unthinkable. I kept arguing with God. The reason that I was on board that crashed aircraft was because I was pursuing my career and heading off to my workplace, which was located in another city—and now God wanted me to leave it. I refused to do so. Nevertheless, His gentle love was proven to be more powerful than the love of this world. God's desire to make my future better was greater than my desire to hold on to my career. With tears, I welcomed His invitation: whatever He wanted me to do, whatever lessons I needed to learn from my trials, whatever things He wanted me to do to please Him. I summed up these with one bold question: "Lord, what are you trying to teach me through this process?"

That beautiful visitation from God changed my motivation. It changed everything about me. His visitation gave me an understanding of the role of questions in my pain and brokenness. I knew that it was okay to ask questions of God, but I just did not know how to ask them from His perspective. My perspective was wrong. I could not figure out where to start and how to ask, because I was so focused on my pain. However, the moment I was willing to show my dependency on Him by asking God, in His wisdom, what He wanted me to do, then God was willing to reason with me. God sees in you something beyond your own understanding, and you must persevere, even if you do not understand. Perseverance will give you godly wisdom and will teach you how to ask.

In that divine moment was a turning point in my journey. I was crying in my bed, telling God that I was sorry for arguing with Him. My wife came to my bed and asked me what happened and why I was crying. I said, "I met Jesus. He spoke to me and told me many things." My wife said, "Have some more sleep. It is still 3am." Oh what a precious moment that was! This was a divine moment that I will never forget. In my pain, Jesus found me and talked to me. God allowed me to ask Him for an explanation from my viewpoint, but God was trying to correct it. His explanation came after I was willing to see my pain from His perspective and His pattern. God wanted me not to bombard Him with "why" questions, but to humble myself willingly to ask, "What does He want me to do?"

The "what" question directed me, and it connected me to the heart of God. The "what" question is totally different from a "why" question. The "what" question enables us to see things from God's standpoint and relates it to the will of God. God reveals a better plan through the "what" questions. The willingness of the heart to align with the will of God is the beginning of a breakthrough. It is a sign of humility that allows God to have His own way.

This is what happened to Gideon when he bombarded God with a lot of "why" questions concerning the suffering of Israel caused by their enemy. God never answered Gideon's "why" questions. Instead, God turned to Gideon and asked him to go and save Israel out of Midian's hand. Gideon did not stay stiff-necked with his why questions, but he went off. Gideon's obedience to go opened a door of protection for Israel. Gideon understood the role of questions in his life. He did not insist that God answer his "why" questions, but Gideon willingly adjusted it to *what* God wanted him to do. Gideon's alignment with God's plan changed the future of Israel forever.

Proverbs 28:14 says, "How blessed is the man who fears always, but he who hardens his heart will fall into calamity (NASB)." It is never too late for God to fix the brokenness of humble ones, but it may be too late for the stiff-necked ones. Solomon's saying is a good reminder: "A man who hardens *his* neck after much reproof will suddenly be broken beyond remedy (Prov 29:1 NASB)." Having the ego to keep pushing God to answer our desired questions is a sign of a hardened heart. However, those who accept the conviction of the Holy Spirit will receive God's grace, mercy, and love without finally experiencing irreplaceable suffering. God uses brokenness to shape us. Brokenness is God's initiative to mend our hearts. Brokenness is a process used by God to deal with us. He may use a gentle way or even a harsh way, but God knows how much we can take. Keep your heart in check, and do not react in anger and bitterness. The divine moment and movement of God not only will come in your peaceful situations, but sometimes they can come through fiery trials and situations. The good news is that God is always ready to turn your course, when you allow yourself to adjust to His will. God never leaves nor forsakes His people, even in times of tribulation and hardship, if they allow themselves to align to His will.

Chapter 4

YOU ARE NOT CONDEMNED

". . . there is now no condemnation for those who are
in Christ Jesus, because through Christ Jesus the law
of the Spirit who gives life has set you free . . ."
(Roma 8:1-2)

M any times, we relate pain and suffering to God being against us, even though we do not know the reason for our suffering. We think that God is mad at us and has condemned us, when we are going through trials and pain. God is not against us when we go through trials. On the contrary, God loves us and is happy with us when everything is going well with us. We must realize that pain and suffering are not things that God does not know.

I was flying to my office that morning, as I normally did once a week or fortnightly. My chauffer, who usually picked me up at the airport, called my wife to tell her that my airplane had not arrived yet. There was news about the crash of the Boeing 737 aircraft at 7:00 a.m. that aired on all local television stations that morning. My chauffer told my wife it was the aircraft that I was on that crashed. All the victims who were still alive, including me, were evacuated from the scene. My wife and my driver, who was supposed to pick me up from the airport, found me dying at the hospital, wrapped in a shroud, and going through a death's-door experience. At the same time, after my accident, my eldest son was admitted to the hospital due to a sudden illness. My world was shattered, and I had every reason to question, "*Why me? Why this?*" But should I have insisted that God answer these "why" questions? I guess that you could say that if the answer would eventually make us feel good, then why not? However, what if the answer is not satisfying, and even makes us feel bad? Should we keep arguing with God about things that we do not understand? I am sure the unending "why" questions can haunt us for the rest of our lives, and there is a possibility of feeling angry toward God and being condemned. Therefore, when we do not understand, we need to trust.

God is not trying to find fault with you in your pain and trials. He is trying to prepare something good out of it, without the influence of others. Even the power of Satan never successfully influences the power and authority of God. You may recall, in the book of Luke, how Satan confronted Jesus in the desert to pressure Him three different times, but to no avail. All that Satan wanted was to tempt Jesus about power. However, Jesus successfully rebutted Satan over power. God just wants us to realize the limits of our humanity, and to acknowledge His transcendent power over us.

Paul recognizes a victory behind the tribulation when he points out: "You may ask me, 'Then why does God still find fault with anybody? For who can resist his will?' On the contrary, who are you—mere man that you are—to talk back to God? Can an object that was molded say to the one who molded it, 'Why did you make me like this?' A potter has the right to do what he wants to with his clay, doesn't he? He can make something for a special occasion or something for ordinary use from the same lump of clay (Rom 9:19-21, ISV)." Paul says that when you keep arguing with God, like "an object that was molded says to the one who molded it, 'Why did you make me like this?'" then it could imply that you reject the intervention of God in your life.

Paul defends the right of God to use certain people to achieve His redemptive plan without having to answer to anyone. God does everything according to His agenda. No one teaches knowledge to God (Job 21:22) This does not mean that God does not have moral principles in His sacred nature when dealing with people. In His nature, God is influenced by His love, mercy, and moral concern (Ps 116:5), and not by human will. God does not arbitrarily choose certain people to be saved and others to remain punished.

God does not try to punish us in the tragedy that causes us to feel guilt and condemnation. David assured us, even when the wicked were intent on putting the righteous to death, that "the LORD will not leave them in the power of the wicked or let them be condemned when brought to trial" (Ps 37:33). Furthermore, Paul explains that there is no condemnation for the believer (Rom 8:1). Your pain and suffering are not a condemnation. Rather, they are a sign of love. God trusts you, and you should trust Him. God is never done with you. God just wanted to say that He has every right over our lives, and He can do whatever He wants to do for our beauty, distinction, and honorable use, even through tragedy, trials, and pains. When God does not condemn us, then we should not feel condemned either. When God does not put blame on us, then we should not put blame on God, or ourselves, either.

When Job was going through many hardships, God did not blame Job. His wife, on the other hand, asked Job to blame God for his pain. Satan used Job's wife to put blame on God, but Job did not blame God. The Scripture says, "In all this, Job did not sin by charging God with wrongdoing (Job 1:22)." Job responded to all the calamities that afflicted him with great sadness, but also with humility and with a submissive attitude toward God, and Job continued to honor God in the midst of great suffering. In his gloomy moments and faltering faith, Job did not turn against God; rather, Job frankly expressed his feelings to God. Job shows us how believers can remain faithful when they face trials in this life, even though they experience great suffering and do not understand it. God will deal with our chaotic feelings and complaints if they are directed at Him not in a rebellious manner, but with sincere trust in Him as a loving God. The Scripture says that God accepted Job's questions, and God finally praised Job for saying what was true about God.

Let us not blame God for what the devil is responsible for. Before you blame God, you need to pause for a moment and ask yourself, "Could these trials come from the enemy to stop me from doing God's plan for my life?" Pausing will give you time to discern the situation. Pausing is a time to connect with God in prayer. In prayer, no blaming and condemnation take place. Prayer is a conversation with God to pour out your heart and to receive His outpouring of love for you. God is watching every aspect of our lives, including our trials. Therefore, when we are crying for help, God immediately says, "I have heard your prayer and seen your tears; I will heal you (2 Kgs 20:5)." God's hand that wipes away every tear is greater than the thousand hands that clapped for your success. This is enough to assure us that God is monitoring our lives.

In prayer, you take your trials to God. However, in condemnation, you take your trials to yourself. Through this pausing moment of prayer, God will assure you that He cannot be tempted by the evil one, and that He Himself does not tempt. Therefore, God assures us, "When tempted, no one should say, 'God is tempting me.' For God cannot be tempted by evil, nor does he tempt anyone (Jas 1:13)." Instead, God promises us that suffering could turn to blessing, as James expresses it, "Blessed is the one who perseveres under trial because, having stood the test, that person will receive the crown of life that the Lord has promised to those who love him (Jas 1:12)."

God might allow us to go through hardships and the wilderness to strengthen our faith, but never to lead us into troubles. God's character shows that He cannot be a source of trouble, and He never uses trouble to condemn us, but to help us. God may appoint troubles and trials for the purpose of discipline and maturity, but God never drowns us in condemnation. Some of you know how it feels when you are swimming in the ocean and suddenly the current of the ocean pulls you down, and you are losing your strength. I guarantee that you immediately will start screaming, "Help me!" hoping that the people on the shore will come to rescue you from your desperate situation. I am also very sure that when the people on the shore hear your screaming for help, that they will not criticize and condemn you first before they come to help you, regardless of the mistake you made by going too far into the dangerous current of the ocean.

In your desperation, God expects to hear from you that you need His help. You need to run to God, instead of running away from Him. God never rejects or condemns you when you run to Him for help. However, God disciplines you, "When you forsake the Lord your God and have no awe of Him (Jer 2:19)." Jeremiah warns that when you leave God feeling condemned, this only causes bitterness and makes you feel like you have lost God's protection and are open to various destructive trials.

When you suddenly feel yourself drowning, this is not a good time to ask "why" questions and to feel condemned. Rather, this is a good time to start shouting at the top of your lungs to get God's attention, just as you would do toward the people on the shore when you are drowning in the ocean. The Bible tells us to, "Call on me in the day of trouble; I will deliver you, and you shall glorify me (Ps 50:15 NRSA)." This is because "Everyone who calls on the name of the Lord will be saved" (Rom 10:13). The reason to call to God in our trouble is because He is constantly listening to our cries.

As soon as my airplane crashed into the rice field, it burst into flames. The passengers were trapped, and a number of passengers perished inside the burning fuselage. Amazingly, I got out through the small window of the airplane and jumped onto the wing. Unfortunately, the wing was flaming with fire and my foot got caught on the wing. I was in big trouble, as I could feel the raging flames burning me. My life hung in the balance, as every second ticked by. The only thing I could do was to shout, "Help me God! Help me!" I shouted because I believe that there was still plenty of God's grace left for me. Indeed, God's grace never runs out for those who cry for help. I successfully dragged my feet free, but I fell headlong into the mud of the rice field and suffered burns on fifty percent of my body. While stuck, I could still smell the burning fuel spewing out from the plane. Fearing the worst, I tried to stand and run away from the burning plane. At this point, I was not aware that I had fallen on my shoulder, resulting in a fracture. While staggering away, I sought help. Sadly, there was not one person who offered to give me help, because all of the passengers were attempting to save themselves (including the pilot and co-pilot, who had already jumped out of the aircraft). Miraculously, a few minutes later, I heard someone shouting in my direction asking me to move slowly. While walking, dragging my foot, I suddenly heard two very loud explosions coming from the direction of the aircraft (as flames engulfed the whole of the fuselage).

Later, I heard that some people, especially the families of the victims, blamed the pilot, the failure of the aircraft engine, and even the shortness of the runway as the causes of the tragedy. Many people had condemning thoughts. Condemnation comes from Satan, and it is meant to tear you down. Condemnation continually points out what a failure you are, and how badly you have messed up. God never tells you what a loser you are when you are drowning in the ocean of tribulation. The devil comes to tear you down, but Jesus comes to build you up. Jesus makes it clear that He came not to condemn the world, but to save it (John 12:47). Jesus is your safe place, and you can go to Him when you are in pain and are suffering, without feeling like you are being condemned. You are not worthless, and you are not a failure. Do not trust your failures. They do not know your future. A successful life is not all about health and wealth or material prosperity. Rather, a successful life is when you know that you are in the center of God's will, and you are at peace with God, even as you go through pain. The God of peace who reigns over you is able to crush the Satan who brought feelings of condemnation.

God is Working on Our Mess

Feeling pain is messy. No one likes a messy life. We would like to see and hope that everything is going in order in our daily lives. And by the way, isn't that what God says, that the steps of good believers are ordered by God (Ps 37:23)?

We like order in life. However, life is not about our likes and our dislikes. Pain does not depend on who chooses to like it or not to like it. If I was given the chance to choose, I would choose not to mess with pain. Unfortunately, we do not choose pain, but pain chooses us. You cannot shift pain to others. You can only bear pain, because God knows you are able to bear it (1 Cor 10:13). You were chosen to bear it for a reason. In the Scripture, the prophet Jeremiah showed that he could not choose not to have pain. From his cry we can see that he was messed up with tribulation, "Heal me, LORD, and I will be healed; save me and I will be saved, for you are the one I praise (Jer 17:14)."

No one asks for healing when he or she is not in pain. Usually, the only reason for a person to see a physician is because he or she needs help healing. When faced with tribulation and persecution, Jeremiah prayed for God's grace to help him carry out his ministry as a prophet. The people and the false prophets had criticized and ridiculed Jeremiah because his prophesies had not been fulfilled. Despite this suffering, Jeremiah refused to leave his ministry, but continued to expect strength and help from God.

The story of Sheila Walsh is worth reading regarding what a messy life means. Sheila, an author and singer, learned from an early age that life is messy. The following story is from her book *In the Middle of the Mess: Strength for This Beautiful, Broken Life.*

Sheila's father, whom she adored, suddenly suffered a brain aneurism and was taken off to intensive care. After a few weeks, her dad came home. He was paralyzed on the left side and could only make sounds. After the accident, her father began to take his anger out on her by spitting in her face or pulling out chunks of her hair. One night, while playing with her sister, Sheila heard her dog growl and looked behind her—her father had his cane raised ready to bring it down on her head. Sheila tried to defend herself, and her father fell to the ground. In that moment, life would never be the same. Her father was taken to an asylum, from which he escaped and ran to the river and drowned himself. Sheila blamed herself for his death and could not wrap her five-year-old brain around how her father previously loved her and then tried to kill her.[1]

The pain inflicted by her earthly father left a wound that Sheila would spend years trying to fix herself. She grew up full of shame, believing that she was a terrible person. She grew up fiercely self-protective and struggled to connect with anyone. She found herself in an endless cycle of anger and sadness. After coming to Christ, Sheila still tried to hide her pain and to pretend that all was well until she came to the end of herself. There, she realized that only her Heavenly Father could truly bring the comfort and peace that she needed in the middle of her mess. Now she encourages others not to be afraid of their brokenness, but rather, to bring it to God, who is big enough to help them through it.[2]

Sometimes, pain can last a long time and cause a messy life. However, once we can break down that wall, it becomes easier, and healing can start. Six months in the hospital and another eight months at home waiting for recovery from my burn wounds was a real messy life for me. The slow recovery of my skin and my fractured shoulder seemed to be unending trials. Many questions continued to haunt my thoughts. Can my skin go back to normal? Can I still have a normal life? Can I still use my crippled finger for work? Am I still able to support my family?

Those thoughts haunted me. One day, I was screaming at the top of my voice. I threw everything that was near me, before my wife ran into my bedroom asking, "What happened?" Oh, I was messed up. I could not help myself anymore. It was so frustrating, as the devil was working hard to pull me down. I hated what had happened to me. I really needed God to give back my joy so I could survive and get through the frustrating times. "Ah, Lord you never allowed the devil to go too far to destroy Job's life, and it won't happen to me either." Truly, God is a powerful wonder-working God. He is not a passive God, and He did not let my cry go unheard, leaving me alone and helpless. When my wife and I prayed for deliverance from bad thoughts, God's peace invaded my life. God saw my pain. He knew my affliction. He heard my cry, even before we started praying for deliverance. God is present in the midst of the center of pain to comfort and to encourage. He shows up when we mess up.

God paid attention to every affliction that Israel was going through, and He was working on it. God assured them through Moses. In Exodus 3:7-10, God said,

> I have indeed seen the misery of my people in Egypt. I have heard them crying out because of their slave drivers, and I am con-

cerned about their suffering. So, I have come down to rescue them from the hand of the Egyptians and to bring them up out of that land into a good and spacious land, a land flowing with milk and honey . . . . And now the cry of the Israelites has reached me, and I have seen the way the Egyptians are oppressing them. So now, go. I am sending you to Pharaoh to bring my people the Israelites out of Egypt.

God spoke to Moses that He was paying attention to the sufferings of His people in Egypt. He also pays attention to the hardships of all His people. God listens to the cries of the hearts and of the oppressed. At such times, God's people should cry out to Him so that He will intervene on their behalf.

Whether our hardships are caused by situations, Satan, or the world, God's comfort, grace, and help are more than adequate to deliver us from all our pains that cause a messy life. God is at work, whether you see Him or not. God never stops fighting for you when you cannot fight for yourself. God knows about your pain, and He is fighting for you as we speak. Do not let your heart be troubled by it. While the Israelites were crying out for help, God was working on their behalf. Do not let your emotions be your decision-maker. Rather, give God a chance to take control over it. The only way that God can show us that He is in control is to put us in situations that we cannot control.

Stop and pray. Let God lead you. He can change your situation. While God is working on your mess, you need to realize that waiting in prayer, and trusting God to do His part, are what He wants from us. When you read the story of David, you will be stunned to see how many times David experienced a messy life: looked down on by his brothers; living in a cold and rough wilderness surrounded by wild animals to tend to his flock; threatened by Goliath; hunted by Saul to be killed; threatened by Absalom, his own son; and he committed adultery with Bathsheba. In all David's mess, one thing that he always did was to come back to God, to be forgiven, cleansed, transformed, and strengthened again.

In His own time, God will put you back together and make you stronger again. Despite trials and hardships, you recover by God's power, because He knows you and He loves you. God understands suffering, and He remembers you in your brokenness. David assures us that God does not ignore brokenness: "The LORD is close to the brokenhearted and saves those who are crushed in spirit" (Ps 34:18). God can clean your mess to give you peace. God even can turn your mess into a message for His glory. He will turn a mess into something amazing. In the last chapter of her book, Sheila Walsh confirms that there is a miracle in the middle of a mess: "When we try to hide our wounds, our scars, our cancers all those things we believe make us less lovely, we make fear and shame the stronghold of our lives. But when we bring our wounds to Christ, when we out our secrets and shame, we make Him the stronghold of our lives, and He uses our wounds for His purposes." God makes something beautiful of us.[3]

God is ready to pick up a messy people to be used. Everything is for His perfect plan and purpose. God is willing to help clean the mess, but you must agree to His conditions. God will not cause pain without allowing something new to be born (Isa 66:9). Birth will bring joy, hope, and order to a messy life.

Pain is to Fulfill God's Plan

You may be very confused, and you may be becoming a pessimistic person when you know that God allows pain to be part of His plan in someone's life. You do not want suffering to be juxtaposed with peace. But wait a minute! I am not saying that God plans to afflict you, nor that you are predestined to be afflicted. What I am saying is that God can use our pain, and that pain is inevitable when God is trying to accomplish His purposes in our lives. It is a fact: life is full of issues and problems. If you study the Bible carefully, then you will find that there is a relationship between pain and gain, and between sorrow and joy. James said, "Count it all joy when you fall into various trials, knowing that the testing of your faith produces patience (Jas 1:2-3 NKJV)." God uses those problems to execute His plan through you. The Scriptures explain it clearly, "'For I know the plans I have for you,' declares the LORD, 'Plans to prosper you and not to harm you, plans to give you hope and a future' (Jer 29:11)."

The believer does not define fate as the world defines it, which is that it makes us feel scared and hopeless. The Bibles does mention predestination, but it is a providence of God that brings hope not hopelessness. Additionally, Jeremiah clearly confirmed a bright future for believers if they cling to God with the right attitude (v. 12). Believers are still going to go through many hardships, trials, or suffering. Israel had to go through the wilderness, but wilderness was not their predestination. Jeremiah assured Israel that God indeed had a good plan for the Israelites, and it was a plan that would give them hope and a prosperous future. However, Israel's suffering was not going to end when they wanted it to end. Their suffering ended according to God's timing.

Many times, when we are stuck with pain and suffering, we become completely focused on waiting for the pain to end. God said that He would fulfill a prosperous future for Israel—after seventy years were completed in Babylon. Israel would not end up in hardship when the requirement of God was fulfilled, their first captivity experience. "This is what the Lord says: 'When seventy years are completed for Babylon, I will come to you and fulfill my good promise to bring you back to this place' (Jer 29:10)."

You see, a better future is not pain-free. Israel had to experience the Babylonian captivity that brought affliction and hardship before God fulfilled His promise to prosper them. Seventy years would form God's purposes for the Israelites. Israel's victory was not the absence of pain. It involved them believing God in order to have enough mental strength to embrace their pain and to learn from it.

Taking a lesson from your current hardship is building a solid foundation for the next storm. Mental strength and a strong faith are keys for endurance. Life must be experienced as a circle. You never will always be on top, and you never will always be down. Therefore, never ask God to free you from pain. It is not going to happen. Suffering, in many ways, remains a mystery, one that we will never fully understand. The mystery belongs to God. Therefore, instead of asking God to free you from the pain, ask God to give you a strong shoulder to carry the pain. God knows that your shoulder has a limit to carrying weight, but if you are willing to lay it upon Him, then He will give you the grace to bear it triumphantly. All trials and problems in your life can be endured with His help and grace. He will free you from all insurmountable burdens, and He will give His rest and comfort to you. Thomas Watson says, "A true Christian finds comfort in God's afflicting rod, 'as sorrowful—yet always rejoicing.'"4

In the Scriptures, the Gospel of Matthew extends a sweet invitation from Jesus to all those who are heavily burdened by saying, "Come to me, all you who are weary and burdened, and I will give you rest (Matt 11:28)." Instead of taking the pain to yourself and becoming a complainer, take it to the Lord in prayer, and He will give you rest. In complaining, you talk to yourself about things that you cannot change. In prayer, you talk to God about things that He can change. God may allow your current pain and trials to continue or even to be heavier than before, just to allow you to see that your real strength, rest, peace, and hope are only found in God, rather than in your current circumstances.

Chapter 26 of Matthew's Gospel describes how Jesus was going through trials. Just before He was arrested, Jesus prayed that the cup would pass from Him (vv. 39, 42). This cup was all the suffering that He was about to endure. In His human nature, Jesus wished to avoid pain and suffering. Just like you and me, in His human nature, Jesus struggled to accept the horrific pain that awaited Him. Notice, however, that in His struggle, Jesus conquered the will of His flesh and submitted to the will of His Father. Jesus made it clear that whatever He would go through, let it be according to God's plan. With willful submission, Jesus said, "My Father, if it is possible, may this cup be taken from me. Yet not as I will, but as you will (Matt 26:39)." Jesus' flesh did not grudge nor murmur complaints in the Garden of Gethsemane, the place of the beginning of pain and suffering. Rather, Jesus prayed for the plan of God to be done. The willful submission of Jesus paid off. His pain, suffering, and death paid all our sin-debts, and victory became ours. God did not do this to His Only Begotten Son without reasons and purposes. All of this was well-planned. Jesus overcame trials, pain, suffering, and death, and He rose again on the third day and lives forevermore (1 Cor 15:4).

What Jesus went through was necessary in order to fulfill God's plan. Even the person who betrayed Jesus was part of God's plan for humanity's victory over pain and suffering because of sin. Jesus could not get to the cross without Judas, the betrayer, Roman soldiers, and the Jewish crowds. Judas gave Jesus a kiss, but it was a kiss that led to Jesus' trials and suffering. The crowds welcomed Jesus when He entered Jerusalem. They took palm branches and went out to meet him, shouting, "'Hosanna!' 'Blessed is he who comes in the name of the Lord!' 'Blessed is the king of Israel!' (John 12:13)." Later, though, these words were used to mock Jesus. Roman soldiers guarded Jesus' tomb after they executed Him.

Who and what caused your pain and hardship today? Maybe someone or something has contributed to your hardship today. However, it was never out of the control of God. All is orchestrated for your own good. Romans 8:28 declares, "And we know that God causes all things to work together for good to those who love God, to those who are called according to His purpose (NASB)." Paul assures us that if everything works for our good, then nothing can be completely bad, because it is always turning out for our good. This verse should always give you hope and comfort that pain is used to fulfill the plan of God. Hold on to God, not to your pain. All people experience pain in life. Let not pain end our lives. Pain will only last temporarily, and we must all walk the journey and the path that God has for our lives. God promises that there is a *purpose* in all pain. We can press on each day knowing that our God loves us and wants to use the hurt and the pain in this world to make us better and not bitter, and to bring Him glory.

Chapter 5

PAIN IS ESSENTIAL

" . . . we know that in all things God works
for the good of those who love him, who have
been called according to his purpose"
(Romans 8:28).

The Merriam-Webster Dictionary defines a sense organ as, " . . . A part of your body (such as your eyes, ears, nose, or tongue) that you use to see, hear, smell, taste, or feel things."[1] Synonyms for sense include feel or feeling. You can feel pain because you have a sense or a feeling. A normal living person can feel pain. It is not normal when you cannot feel the heat or the cold. Painlessness is often sought physically, emotionally, and spiritually. Many people try to avoid pain. For example, childbirth is associated with pain, as well as the fear or anxiety of mothers. Therefore, a modern medical treatment is trying to avoid the childbirth pain by performing a Cesarean section (C-section). A C-section is perceived as an escape from labor pain, and it has become prevalent among women who voluntarily choose C-section as the preferred mode of delivery. (However, C-sections are also used for medical reasons.) Another example of avoiding pain is to die without feeling pain due to terminal illnesses, which involves euthanasia. This practice has become prevalent in many societies today, whether it is requested by the dying person himself/herself or by the family. Whether it is a legal or an illegal practice, the process to speed up death is for the purpose of relieving the patient's pain and suffering.

Many people try various ways to avoid pain. The fact is that everyone will experience pain, and it does not matter who you are. The majority of women know that childbirth will be painful, yet women still get pregnant. Many people go through terminal illnesses, yet they do not hasten to take their own lives. When people are single, they see married couples having many troubles and problems, yet people still get married and raise children. If everybody really lives to avoid pain, then nobody would get married. Nevertheless, people get married all the time. Nearly two hundred years ago, Thomas Jefferson wrote, 'The art of life is the avoiding of pain.' When we first hear that statement, it appears to be true. None of us deliberately looks for pain as we go about our daily life. All of us do our best to avoid pain, but pain is an important part of our spiritual development.[2] Without the dark, you will never see the stars. Without pain, you will never expect healing.

A story on the NBC News website about Ashlyn Block, daughter of John and Tara Blocker, is worth reading. Their story is not about how their daughter suffers from a painful disease. Rather, it is about how their daughter cannot feel pain. Ashlyn suffers from a congenital insensitivity to pain with anhidrosis, or CIPA—a rare genetic disorder that prevents her brain from receiving signals that she's experiencing pain. CIPA is a rare disorder, affecting only about seventeen people in the United States, and about 100 people worldwide. This and other related genetic disorders affect the autonomic nervous system—which controls blood pressure, heart rate, sweating, the sensory nerve system, and the ability to feel pain and temperature. The pain loss is so severe that they can injure themselves repetitively, and they can actually mutilate themselves because they do not know when to stop. The pain loss can be deadly, featuring an impaired immune response to infection, which can cause early death. People with CIPA cannot feel pain, and this is extremely dangerous.[2]

Suffice to say, if we never felt pain when something was wrong in our bodies, then we would be more susceptible to death. Pain is beneficial to our lives. Pain is not in vain. If you do not have pain, then you cannot take the heat. We should thank God for pain because it alerts us that something is wrong in our bodies. When there is no pain, then a person tends not to reach out for help, because the person thinks that he or she does not need help. Physically, pain will help us know when we need medical attention. Spiritually, pain will help us develop perseverance. Allow yourself to feel pain and do not deny it. But ask God to heal you and to make you stronger. When you feel pain, it means you are a normal human, and you are running your race. It is not a sign of lack of faith, but it is a sign of breakthrough. Pain is a sign that you are still alive and, therefore, you can feel it. Life is between the points of conception/birth and death, and no one experiences a pain-free life in between those points.

David Jeremiah says, "Character and substance are shaped in the crucible of adversity. Show me someone who lives a carefree life with no problem or trials or dark nights of the soul, and I'll show you a shallow person. . . . Unless there is pain in the formula, we will never stop to listen carefully to what [God] is saying."[4] Character is mostly shaped by a problem or a hardship, and not by a good situation or pleasure. Pain increases our dependency on God.

James expresses the benefit of pain, "Consider it pure joy, my brothers and sisters, whenever you face trials of many kinds, because you know that the testing of your faith produces perseverance (Jas 1:2-3)". James says that when we endure painful trials, then we can take joy in knowing that God is at work in us to produce endurance and Christ-like character. If you have never had trials, you can never know this joy. James mentions these various trials as tests of our faith. Trials sometimes afflict us so that God can test the sincerity of our faith. The Bible never teaches that difficulties in life always indicate that God is not happy with us. God uses those trials to toughen us and to make us grow. The way to grow is to make progress. Pain is used by God to make progress.

Rejecting pain only causes you to be frustrated and to bring you down. Let yourself feel the pain. Your current pain will overcome your vulnerability to worse pain and will allow you to recognize pain when you come out of it. If you never felt pain, then you would never appreciate healing. If you never had a trial, then you would never fully cherish the comfort of God. If you never were in trouble, then you would never fully acknowledge the grace and mercy of God who rescued you from that trouble.

To be able to truly recognize and appreciate healing, you need to experience the opposite end of the spectrum. Persevering in pain enables you to enjoy your rewards more than before. Part of what made the Israelites survive for forty years in the wilderness was the hardships that they went through as slaves and being treated badly in Egypt. The trials that they experienced in Egypt were preparation for their next trials in the wilderness. The trials that they had, both in Egypt and in the wilderness, were important lessons for them to appreciate their freedom and their eventual victory in the Promised Land. Pain does not mean that you have failed. Pain simply means that you are a human being who runs the race. Pain will make you appreciate your next healing in a way that you never knew before. Pain is essential, and it has its own purposes.

Pain Reveals What You are Made of

Pain and suffering are not meant to fail you, but to reveal you. Pain and suffering draw out the true attitudes and desires of the heart. A right attitude will be composure, but a wrong attitude will bring agitation. God knows everything in our hearts. God is in control of all human circumstances.

In the account of Job, the devil could do nothing to Job without asking permission from God. Before Job was struck with pain, Satan asked God's permission to afflict Job, and God gave permission to Satan. This was to prove that God was in control. "So, Satan went out from the presence of the LORD and afflicted Job with painful sores from the soles of his feet to the crown of his head (Job 2:7)." Although Satan has no authority apart from God, Satan is active in causing pain. Satan will not come against us if we are already going in the same direction as him, because we are on his side. However, if we ever bump against Satan, this means that we are going in the same direction as God, and God will be there both with and for us.

God gave permission to Satan to attack Job. Satan's attacks showed what Job was made of. People react in different ways to pain. Either they turn to God, or they turn against Him. When attacked, a strong believer will run to God, not run from God. A non-believer (or even a weak believer) will turn away from or turn against God. When hit by pain, a strong believer gets better, and not bitter. How you respond makes all the difference.

When everything is going well in life, sometimes the identity that we display is false. In easy circumstances, it is easy to live out of a false identity. Pain will tell our true identity. In pain, God often speaks to us concerning who we really are in His eyes. However, God never uses pain to obscure our identity, but rather to confirm our identity. Our identity in Christ shall never be falsified by pain. The devil, on the other hand, is trying to confuse you concerning your identity by getting you not to accept who you are, and the devil accuses you as a bad person when pain hits you.

Satan's attack also showed what Job's wife was made of. As soon as Satan attacked Job, his wife told him to reject God and get it over with. Satan's attack displayed her identity. It seems doubtful that Job's wife was a true believer. When her husband was in trouble, she spoke harshly to Job by saying "Are you still maintaining your integrity? Curse God and die! (Job 2:9)." She got bitter, not better, when trials hit her own family. She could not accept the reality of life. Job, in contrast, did not blame God for the trials that he was going through (Job 1:22). Pain and suffering revealed the characters of Job and his wife. We have just seen two different responses to trials.

The Job narrative reveals two types of people when pain strikes. One becomes lost in the storm of life. The other becomes anchored and saved. One is dependent upon himself or herself, taking things into one's own hands and believing in one's own thinking. The other places his or her trust in God and believes in His promises. One is afraid and giving up. The other is courageous enough to face the storm. One accepts the lies of Satan and lives in them. The other rejects Satan's lies and lives in God's truth. Job's wife became lost in believing her own thinking, trusted Satan's lies, and gave up in the circumstances. Therefore, she fell apart and became bitter. She caused injury rather than remedy to her husband because that was what she was made of. Job, however, who believed in God and rejected the lies of Satan, became better and Job was said to have received a double blessing later.

Pain and suffering do not create character. Rather, they reveal and develop character. Job, a man acquainted with much pain, stated, "Man, who is born of woman, is short-lived and full of turmoil (Job 14:1 NASB)." Unlike his wife, Job realized that man is born for trouble, and he did not deny it. Instead, Job gave a godly response to his pain.

Spending six months in the hospital and another eight months lying at home from severe burns was truly painful. However, having someone around who cared for and loved me was truly a blessing. I was grateful to God for my wife, who was willing to take care of me and who prayed for me, even through tears, during my affliction. Every day, we held our hands in prayer. Together, we faced our storm and put our faith in God for healing. We acknowledged that the storm was allowed by God for a purpose in our marriage and family. As couples, we do not just hold each other's hands when we feel joy, but also when we fall apart, like Job's wife, when storms strike. As married couples, we all made promises before God that nothing would tear us apart—not trials, sickness, nor affliction—because the God who carried Job through his pain is the same God who would sustain us. If you are a couple, then let this be a reminder to you that the same loving God is also present in your marriage as you go through the storms of life.

People may have different attitudes toward the storms of life, but we must build our lives on a solid foundation for when the storms strike. The Bible says that the character of a person determines what kind of house he or she will build against storms. In the book of Matthew, we read:

Therefore, everyone who hears these words
of mine and puts them into practice is like
a wise man who built his house on the rock.
The rain came down, the streams rose, and
the winds blew and beat against that house;
yet it did not fall, because it had its foundation on the rock. But everyone who hears
these words of mine and does not put them
into practice is like a foolish man who built
his house on sand. The rain came down, the
streams rose, and the winds blew and beat
against that house, and it fell with a great
crash. (Matt 7:24-27)

The first man was foolish and built his house on sandy
soil, where it was easy to dig the foundation, and he probably
finished it in a short time. The second man was wise and
built his house on a rocky hill, where it was hard to dig the
foundation, and he probably needed a longer time to build it.
When a storm broke upon the houses, the first man's house
was swept away. However, the second man's house was safe
and remained. How we endure the storms of life shows what
we have built our lives on. The house that we build describes
our character. Character is part of personality. Having a
strong personality does not mean that the person will face
greater storms while a weaker personality faces lesser storms.
The storms never single-out which person to hit. However,
the strong person will always survive. The strong person cannot be intimidated by a storm but remains standing solid in

the midst of the stormy circumstances. The response to the storms all depends on what kind of person you are.

Many people are trying to stand against storms based on their own self-reasoning. Today, we can see people build their houses with sophisticated materials only to find themselves in shaky houses, shaky marriages, shaky relationships with co-workers, or shaky emotions. A solid house is not about the sophisticated materials that it is made of. Rather, it is about the foundation on which the house will stand. People who are trying to build their own lives using wrong spiritual tools will cause their spiritual lives to crumble. People with strong spiritual character do not depend on what they have, but on Who has them. These strong people experience shakiness in life, but they know that God is for them and with them. The word of God is their strong foundation. They know that while they are building their lives upon the word of God, that God is helping them build their lives on solid ground. God builds them with His powerful word that outlasts the storms. Paul said, "Do you not know that your body is the temple (the very sanctuary) of the Holy Spirit Who lives within you? (1 Cor 6:19 AMPC)." Paul convinced us that our bodies are the sanctuary of God, and He wants these built strong based on His word, and not based on weak character or fear.

The word of God is the sure foundation on which we should build our spiritual lives, and when pain and suffering come—and they will—we will not buckle, bend, or bow. The sand represents your emotions that can sway you toward bad feelings, but the solid rock is what you choose to think and do, even if it does not feel good. The result will keep you on the solid rock's ground. What kind of storm are you going through? A storm in your marriage or relationship, financial issues, or disease? All of these can shake your life, but life that is built on the solid rock will remain firm in times of storm.

The foundation on which you build your life is the only thing that will last when the storm hits. The storm ultimately will come. It is not a question of if, but when. In Matthew 8:23-27, we read about people of faith, whom we call the disciples of Jesus, who lived with Him every day and who listened to Him talk. However, one day when Jesus asked them to go over to the other side of the lake, they went through a fierce storm. The Scripture affirms that we cannot be free of the storms of life—we still have them (2 Tim 3:12). We cannot be storm-free, but we can be storm-proof. Therefore, Jesus taught that there is another way to live—a better way. He wants us to build the house of our lives on His rock-hard foundation so that we can be unshakeable in the midst of unstable circumstances, and we can smile in the storm.

God is not only the solid foundation on whom we can stand strong in times of storms, trials, or tragedies, but He is also the shelter for protection from the stinging of the heat. The psalmist says,

> Whoever dwells in the shelter of the Most High will rest in the shadow of the Almighty. I will say of the LORD, "He is my refuge and my fortress, my God, in whom I trust." Surely, he will save you from the fowler's snare and

from the deadly pestilence. He will cover you
with his feathers, and under his wings you
will find refuge; his faithfulness will be your
shield and rampart. (Ps 91:1-4).

The wise person will choose to take refuge in the safest shelter, not in a crumbling shelter poorly made by man. The Psalm 91 reveals the security of people who fully rely on God; we are assured that God will be our protection, and that we can seek His protection in times of spiritual and physical danger.

This storm that you are facing is a personal revealer to you. Many people have chosen a wrong shelter to protect themselves from the storm, but to no avail. A man named Tim said that he had made many wrong choices in order to feel like he had friends. As a teen, he was extremely shy, and he desperately longed for friends and a social life. In an attempt to satisfy his desires, he made poor choices and he did appalling things that will remain unmentioned. Tim hung out with the wrong crowd, and he started cursing and drinking. His so-called friends only hung out with him because he looked old enough to buy liquor for them. All he managed to accomplish was to alienate the few real friends that he did have, which left him that much more lonely. Tim's so-called friends offered him hard drugs, and he became rebellious against his parents. He admitted that he had put himself in great peril and dangers that caused him a stormy life. However, at twenty-seven years old, Tim attended an evangelistic meeting with a friend who had come out of his own rebellion, and who had turned to God. As Tim sat down on the first row, he felt a definite knocking on his heart. He opened the door of his heart to Jesus Christ, and Tim has never been the same since. Tim had an opportunity to come out from the crumbling shelter. He found the perfect shelter because he made a right choice when he was in the mire. God removed Tim's stony, rebellious heart, and put a new heart in Tim.[5] You see, like Tim, each one of us has a storm of life that crumbles us. But through trials, we can learn that no storm is too big to prevent God from saving us. God is present in our storms.

Pain Helps Us Grow

God knows the trials that are ahead of us before we even go through them, yet God nudges us along, and so we move along. We cannot be stagnant. Growth is a must for everyone. Pain and suffering can be a good and powerful tool for growth, if we handle these faithfully and effectively. No parent feels happy to see that their precious children did not grow. The process of growing goes through many stages. Remember when your children had their first teeth, they cried a lot, and they did not want to drink the milk you gave them. Remember when they first rode on a bicycle? They failed and fell many times, and often they bled. Growth often means pain. Without that pain, they would not be who they are today.

This is how faith is: it is often like growing pains. To grow requires a degree of pain and suffering. When faith is tested in a battleground, it often grows stronger to endure in a greater capacity. Life is not a playground, but a battleground. Every one of us should take action to win the battle, but action without faith will kill us in the battleground. Therefore, faith must correspond with action. This takes our faith from the realm of theory to reality so we can start living out our faith and becoming mature in facing the real world. Everyone has battles to fight in life. These battles are proof that we do not only live in the realm of theory.

A. B. Simpson, founder of The Christian and Missionary Alliance, said,

> Temptation exercises our faith and teaches us to pray. It is like military drill and a taste of battle to the young soldier. It puts us under fire and compels us to exercise our weapons and prove their potency. It shows us the resources of Christ and the preciousness of the promises of God. . . . Every victory gives us a new confidence . . . and new courage for the next onset of the foe, so that we become not only victors, but more than conquerors, taking the strength of our conquered foes and gathering precious spoil from each new battlefield. So that temptation strengthens what we have received and establishes us in all our spiritual qualities and graces.[6]

When Job's life fell, he showed an attitude of maturity in the act of surrendering, and he praised the name of the Lord! Job did not say, "I cannot believe it," but he simply trusted the Lord with his pain (Job 1:21-22).

Waiting on my healing process from the severe burns from the airplane crash, for almost one and a half years, was truly a hard thing for me. However, what made it even harder was that I had to quit my job. When God asked me to leave my job, I refused to do so because I feared what the future might hold. Inflicted with severe pain, in financial difficulties, and being asked to leave my job were truly troublesome and unthinkable for me. I could not contain my emotions. It was too much to bear. However, I already made a vow in that hospital to leave my job, when I heard God ask me to do so. I could not play games with God and break the vow that I made that night when God visited me. God really reminds us not to break our vows: "If you make a vow to the LORD your God, do not be slow to pay it, for the LORD your God will certainly demand it of you, and you will be guilty of sin (Deut 23:21)." A vow to the Lord, once made, is to be kept, and God requires it. But how?

I was facing real life—it was not hallucination. The scars all over my body were real. The damage to my shoulder was real, and the doctor said that it would never be fully recovered. The pain that I went through was terribly real. And the job that I held on to so dearly was lost. It was real. I was heading off to a battleground, not to a playground. As soon as I left the hospital and was finally healed, I did not go back to my former work as Chief Tax District. Nor did I get my usual beautiful paycheck. Instead, the Lord asked me to go to the field to do ministry, taking my wife and four children without a paycheck. My colleagues ridiculed me for leaving a good job and position, and worldly friends were distant. I thought, "Lord, are you kidding?" I was full of uncertainty, but I had to embrace it. The pain was real, but it helped me grow emotionally and spiritually, and it shaped my life. I knew that the future of my family was not depending on my paycheck, nor on temporary friendships in this world. I knew that I must grow, even in the midst of pressures, because I had made my commitment to serve God as soon as I got healed.

My experience was nothing compared to the many afflictions that Paul had gone through: forsaken by friends, imprisoned, and persecuted by the Roman Empire. Paul described these as if God had put a thorn in his flesh (2 Cor 12:7). Having a thorn in the flesh is like pain that is never ending. Like it or not, though, you must bear it daily. Bearing a heavy burden on a shoulder is for people who are willing to chew hard foods, not for the people who just want to drink milk. Spiritual maturity is required to chew these hard foods. The thorn is to make you feel the existence of real pain, as well as to show the real you. Like a thorn, pain will continue to occur, but if you knew how to handle it, it would no longer be a problem. The thorn will not break you down. The thorn might be burdensome. However, it is not the thorn that pulls you down, but the way you carry the thorn. Pain is not a condition, but your attitude against the pain is.

The thorn that Paul refers to conveys the idea of pain, hardship, suffering, brokenness, or physical weakness. Paul's thorn was given to prevent him from being arrogant, and to make him more dependent on divine grace. Consider what Paul said: "And He has said to me, 'My grace is sufficient for you, for power is perfected in weakness.' Most gladly, therefore, I will rather boast about my weaknesses, so that the power of Christ may dwell in me (2 Cor 12:9-10 NASB)." Paul recognized that God's grace was being given to him so that he could endure pain. Therefore, in confidence Paul declares that, " . . . For Christ's sake, I delight in weaknesses, in insults, in hardships, in persecutions, in difficulties. For when I am weak, then I am strong (2 Cor 12:11b)."

We might ask: How in the world can weakness make one strong? David Jeremiah illustrates it as follows: "Years ago, a TV commercial advertised a glue with the claim that when it repaired a broken object, the point of repair would be stronger than any other part of the object. Under stress, it would break anywhere else before breaking the bond of the glue. That's what God did for Paul. He filled Paul's broken place with His own strength, so that Paul was stronger in his weak place than anywhere else."[7]

In pain and brokenness, you are being repaired with the glue of God, with His most powerful energy to strengthen you again. Brokenness is an opportunity to experience the grace of God. God will give you the grace to bear pain to experience spiritual growth. Whenever we face trials and temptations, this is the grace given to us to be able to say, like James, "Consider it pure joy, my brothers and sisters, whenever you face trials of many kinds, because you know that the testing of your faith produces perseverance. Let perseverance finish its work so that you may be mature and complete, not lacking anything (Jas 1:2-4)."

God wants to perfect you through pain and suffering, and He is working on it. Let God do His part, and you make yourself available even as you go through trials. You must face all this with joy, because testing will develop steadfast faith, mature character, and mature expectations. The signs of firm faith are praising God in pain and thanking Him through suffering. Our faith can only reach full maturity when we are faced with difficulties and challenges. James mentions that these various trials are, " . . . Testing of your faith." Temptations sometimes afflict us so that God can test the sincerity of our faith. The Bible never teaches that difficulties in life indicate that God is not happy with us. Such difficulties can be a sign that God acknowledges our commitment to Him.

Yan T. Wee puts it like this: "This imperfect world is the perfect place for God to try our hearts, mold us into His likeness, and bless us with the desires of our hearts as we trust and obey Him till the end."[8] Wee adds, "Before every believer in Christ lies two approaches to suffering: one, to see nothing good in it and loathe it; and the other, to see beyond suffering the divine purpose of God and profit from it. The first will consign him to a life of endless misery and regret, while the latter will free him to grow and gain in his God-ordained tribulation, which is designed for his good."[9]

Those who are weak and not mature in faith do not have sensitivity and spiritual wisdom concerning what is good and what is evil in life. On the contrary, people who have trained their senses to endure hardship will be more mature in life. Paul remarks that pain and suffering can lead to spiritual growth and produce positive character in those who endure (Rom 5:3-4). Pain helps mature us in our practical lives. God uses pain as a training tool. He lovingly and faithfully uses pain to develop personal righteousness, maturity, and our walk with Him.

Pain Prepares Us for a Special Task

I did not understand why the storm hit and brought me pain. My intention was just to go to my workplace that morning, and it happened to be in another city. So, I boarded the airplane. However, I found myself dying in the hospital, and it was my last work trip and the end of my career. No wonder I was asking God "why" questions. Most of the time, we tend to succumb to our current situations, and we are unable to see beyond our current situations. If you knew that your pain was preparing you for a better life, you would not complain. But whether you knew it or not does not matter, because God will use your pain for a special task. It is all for the best plan of God. Whenever you think that you are done, God is not done with you. If you feel that way, then read the chorus of the following song:

God's not done with you
Even with your broken heart and your
wounds and your scars
God's not done with you
Even when you're lost and it's hard and you're
falling apart
God's not done with you
It's not over, it's only begun
So don't hide, don't run
Cause God's not done with you.[10]

God never gives up on you, even when you give up on Him. You can count on God. The storm may take you by surprise, but it cannot take God by surprise. Because God, the maker of heaven and earth, is in control of the storm and of your life, and God never takes His eyes off you. Paul assures us that God remains faithful, because He cannot deny Himself (2 Tim 2:13). God trusts you, and you should trust Him. He is preparing you for a special task to impact others.

In Genesis 37, we read the beginning narrative about Joseph that proves that his pain and suffering were only preparing him for a special task. The jealous brothers who cast Joseph into a pit to finish off his life were only preparing Joseph for a special assignment that, ultimately, would give Joseph and his family a better life. Much adversity prepared Joseph for the task ahead. After being abandoned by his brothers and removed from his people, Joseph was still able to say that God did it! But why did God do it? As Joseph said, all of it was, " . . . To save many people alive (Gen 50:20

NKJV)." And to save his family, who were suffering during the great drought. Joseph was brought out of the pit to the palace of Pharaoh. When you are in the pit of pain, God is there, and you are going to make it out, and you are going to come out of your pit prepared for a noble task in the next page of your life. If God asks you to put something down, it is because God wants you to pick up something greater. Just because you were in a pit does not mean that you will never go to the palace to secure others. You may have not realized it, but your pit is a valuable preparation for your elevation. Even Judas was used by God to betray Jesus, but it was a preparation for Jesus to be exalted.

You need to know that the experiences of your life can and will be used by God to help others. And when you have suffered, you can offer a special measure to someone else who is suffering. When you experience much, you can give much. A life that does not suffer can only provide a little comfort to people who are suffering. When you experience pain, pain will shape your personality. Your sympathy toward others was borne out of experience. Your pain experience will enable you to share with others who face similar troubles. Sympathy comes from pain. The pain that you may currently be experiencing will one day be worth it. God does not waste experiences.

If you just found out that someone has cancer, and you are a cancer survivor, then your heart will be triggered to give comfort to that person. A burn survivor, like me, has sympathy toward my fellow burn survivors, because I have experienced it. If parents just had a child die and feel as though they cannot go on another minute, then if you have been down that road, you can comfort those parents like no one else. After your current pain, God will give you an ear to hear someone else crying in pain, as well as wisdom to comfort the hurting, and a hand to help people in need. A. W. Tozer sums it up in these words, "It is doubtful whether God could ever bless a man greatly until He has hurt him deeply."[11] Your passion and compassion toward others is birthed from your pain and suffering, and God wants you to impact your world with it. The Scripture says, "I will be a Father to you, and you will be my sons and daughters, says the Lord Almighty (2 Cor 6:18)."

Paul reminds us that pain has noble purposes. In 2 Corinthians 1:4–5, Paul says that, "He comforts us in all our troubles so that we can comfort others. When others are troubled, we will be able to give them the same comfort God has given us. You can be sure that the more we suffer for Christ, the more God will shower us with His comfort through Christ (NLT)." Pain has its goal. In the many difficulties that he experienced, Paul learned that there is no pain and suffering, even though it may be great, that can separate believers from the love (care and mercy) of their heavenly Father (Rom 8:35-39). Sometimes, God allows difficulties to affect our lives so that we, after experiencing His comfort, can comfort others in their difficulties. Pain that you experience in this life takes on new meaning. It is a means through which God works to accomplish His purposes in your life. It is a means to shape you to display God's character. God's purposes are not always your immediate wealth, health, or comfort, but your character.

Paul says that those whom, "God foreknew he also predestined to be conformed to the image of his Son, that he might be the firstborn among many brothers and sisters (Rom 8:29)." All that we go through in this world, good or bad, is a tool used by God in order for us to be conformed to the image of Christ, His character. Pain is a tool that is shaping each person's character to become a better, humble, loving, and useful person for God. Pain is a preparation for a new beginning—a new assignment. Suffering brings real pain, but it is not an end. God uses pain to toughen us up and to get us ready to do the things that He calls us to do. Such pain can be a sign that God acknowledges our commitment to Him. Paul went through it. Therefore, he said in his own words:

> We *are* troubled on every side, yet not distressed; we *are* perplexed, but not in despair; persecuted, but not forsaken; cast down, but not destroyed; always bearing about in the body the dying of the Lord Jesus, that the life also of Jesus might be made manifest in our body. . . . So then death worketh in us, but life in you. . . . For which cause we faint not; but though our outward man perish, yet the inward *man* is renewed day by day (2 Cor 4:8-10, 12, 16 KJV).

Jesus wants us to manifest His compassion to people around us. The hurting world needs healing, and He is using your sickness to strengthen the sick, your pain for peace, and your test for a testimony in order to encourage others and to show that there is a turning point in life. Your reaction to someone's trials determines how God is going to react to your trial when you go through it. Be willing to help others in their trials. God will give you an opportunity to reap what you sow. Your special task is to make Jesus manifest to the world. Your next level is being manifested through your pain, and you are being prepared to embrace your next assignment. God can take a broken piece and He is ready to use it. Your pain is not an accident; rather, it is arranged for the greater purpose of helping others.

The Bible tells us many stories of how God used people out of trials and hardships. The life journey of Joseph from the pit to the prison, and from prison to the palace, was real and encouraging (Gen 41:1-57). The life story of Job included loss of property and children, in horrible illness, despised by his wife, and mocked by his friends—but the Lord restored his fortunes and gave him twice as much as he had before (Job 42:10-12). Job's life encouraged his brothers and sisters and all who knew him. Many people in the Bible and around us were used by God through their pain to impact others, and you are one of them. God does not choose you just by random luck. He knows you well.

You may go through trials and hardships, but God is going to use you to be a vessel to fulfill His mission through your pain. God uses the worst of us to reach the rest of us.

He is using your afflictions to soothe the afflicted. Do not give up! Keep your faith and keep your belief. There are a thousand reasons for living. God has so much more for your life. Despite trials and hardships, you can be used by God. Because He knows you, and He is willing to tell you His plans and His calling.

Chapter 6

WHAT WAS MEANT FOR EVIL, GOD MEANT FOR GOOD

"You intended to harm me, but God intended it for good to accomplish what is now being done, the saving of many lives"
(Genesis 50:20)

There is nothing else that the devil wants from you but to see you staggering in the wilderness, crushed in trials, and frustrated daily in your life. Lisa Bevere writes, "The devil is compared to a roaring lion on the lookout for someone to devour. . . . He consumes our joy, our peace, our rest, our strength, as well as our health, our relationships, and our thoughts."[1] The devil has a scheming plan for you, and he wants to confront you with this. Jesus, the Son of God, knows this, because the devil did this to Him. Therefore, Jesus reminds us: "The thief comes only to steal and kill and destroy; I have come that they may have life and have it to the full" (John 10:10). The devil wants to destroy your health, your happiness, your finances, and your marriage.

The devil is the thief who just wants to ruin everything that he can get his hands on. He can get his hands on your body, mind, and heart, and he takes what he wants before you even recognize his presence. He is a stealer of your blessing in very cunning and deceptive ways. The devil also comes to kill. He wants you to give up your blessed and joyful life and surrendered to him and his will, simply because he does not want you to have a blessed and joyful life. The final thing that the devil wants to do is to destroy you. He wants to annihilate you totally, and to make you feel defeated. What a miserable feeling the devil causes in life.

There is no doubt that the schemes of the devil are to make you be in pain, feel depressed, and struggle through your entire life. Many people have experienced the schemes of the devil that cunningly target us, and you are not alone. I was one of them. Waiting for the healing process of my burn wounds seemed like an unending hardship to me—and that was a good time to be used by the devil to feel intimidated. The devil confronted me and accused me of making mistakes by flying on that morning, and therefore, I deserved what happened. My mind was being intimidated, and I wanted to jump out of my bed, even though I was still bound to my bed. Unable to move and feeling frustrated, I screamed, and I threw everything that I could reach in my bedroom. Oh, what is wrong with me! My wife ran to my room, scared. However, my wife prayed for me, and I was delivered from that intimidation.

It is no doubt that the devil means to make you feel helpless and frustrated. The devil's work is to prevent your victory and to make you a victim. He laughs when you are bitter, and he is mocked when you are better. His schemes are to devour your life in order to keep you from your victory. Peter, one of Jesus' disciples and a close friend, had been there. Therefore, Peter reminds that God calls us to, " . . . Be alert and of sober mind," watching out for the schemes of the devil who, " . . . Prowls around like a roaring lion looking for someone to devour (1 Pet 5:8)." The devil uses many things, including people around you, to achieve his goals.

Job was mocked by people around him—his close friends—not because he was ungodly, but because he was, in fact, very godly. Job was the most suffering person after Jesus, as scholars say. Job's three friends were not able to endure the mystery of his suffering, so they blamed and mocked him. His first friend, Eliphaz, put the blame on Job himself. In Job 4:7-8, Eliphaz said, "Think now, who that was innocent ever perished? Or where were the upright cut off? As I have seen, those who plow iniquity and sow trouble reap the same (NRSV)."

"Job's second friend, Bildad, says much the same. 'See, God will not reject a blameless person nor take the hand of evildoers (Job 8:20).' The third friend, Zophar," mocked him even harsher by saying, "'If iniquity is in your hand, put it far away, do not let wickedness reside in your tents. Surely then you will lift up your face without blemish; you will be secure and will not fear. . . . Your life will be brighter than the noonday (Job 11:14-15, 17).'"[2]

Job's afflictions were real. Therefore, he expressed this with a broken heart, "Why then did you bring me out of the womb? I wish I had died before any eye saw me. If only I had never come into being or had been carried straight from the womb to the grave! (Job 10:18-19)." It was literally unbearable. Therefore, he wished that he had never existed. To make it even worse, his three friends judged him, rather than becoming agents of God's compassion to him, even though they lacked a basis for judging him. His three friends practiced vigilante justice in God's name. And with one voice they basically said, "Job, you got what you deserved." Job's friends gave in to this judgmental practice as though they knew the reason for his pain and suffering. How much harm have well-intentioned close friends caused by giving pious-sounding answers to suffering, even though we have no idea what we're talking about? Indeed, their rhetoric becomes increasingly hostile, blaming Job for his pain and suffering. The three friends became a self-appointed judges who placed the blame on Job and defended God, as if they knew God's plan for Job's life.[3]

The three friends become hell-bent (literally, given Satan's role) on defending God by placing the blame on Job.[4] The brothers of Joseph had given in to Satan's role to end Joseph's life. Satan knew Joseph's potential, and he was trying to prevent Joseph from getting his promotion by using his brothers' scheme to crush his dreams in the pit. The jealous rivals of Daniel were used by Satan to ask King Darius to throw Daniel into the lion's den to stop Daniel from being a successful Jew in the imperial kingdom. Saul had been jealous of David sometimes. Saul heard a group of ladies who gave more credit to David, and Saul knew that his son Jonathan loved David. Saul realized David's abilities, success, and popularity in the eyes of God's people. Jealousy grew in Saul's heart and caused him to harm David. All these schemes had been used by Satan through close friends and family for evil, which caused pain and suffering.

Why Satan Did It

In Hebrew, Satan means adversary, and he was the superhuman adversary of Job and of his people Israel.[5] He was a good angelic prince. He was appointed to serve the throne of God, but he rebelled and became a great enemy of God and mankind (Ezek 28:12-15). Satan and many of his angels then were thrown to the earth and the space around them, where they have been carrying out their work to destroy the lives of humans—but not without the permission of God. Why is the devil fighting hard to destroy you? Because he is afraid of who you truly are!

Job's three friends became hell-bent, used by Satan, to destroy Job's life by blaming him for his pain. However, God used Job's pain to bless his life and the people around him. Satan had been cast out of Heaven, but he still had access to the throne of God. Satan even dared to come into God's presence and to talk to God about his plan to destroy Job's life, and Satan asked God to punish Job (Job 1:6-12). Jesus himself was led by the Spirit into the wilderness to be tempted by the devil (Matt 4:1). The temptation of Jesus by Satan was an attempt to deflect Jesus from the perfect path of obedience to

God's will. Satan wanted Jesus to fail in achieving God's plan that the Father had purposed through Jesus' life. Satan is our biggest enemy.

Satan asked God to curse Job on his behalf. Listen to Satan's request: " . . . Stretch out your hand and strike everything he has, and he will surely curse you to your face (Job 1:11)." Satan goes before God to make accusations against us and to destroy us, but God knows what Satan is doing. God knew that Job was a righteous man. God praised Job, and said to Satan's face: "Have you considered my servant Job? There is no one on earth like him; he is blameless and upright man, a man who fears God and shuns evil (Job 1:8)." God's words indicate that at this point, Job's character was summed up in blamelessness.

Later, though, Satan was allowed to put his hand on Job (Job 2:4-7). Joseph was in a dark pit, after all. Daniel was thrown into the lions' den, no matter what. David was hunted and threatened to be killed at any cost. Why? Because Satan wanted Job to be sick with painful sores, in addition to having been afflicted by the loss of his children and his livestock. Satan wanted Joseph to be depressed and miserable. Satan wanted Daniel to be devoured and shattered. Satan wanted David to be defeated and to fail to be a king of Israel. Satan knew that once they gave up, the battle would be lost.

Satan is a deceiver and the accuser of the brethren (Rev 12:10). Satan accused Joseph of being a false dreamer. Satan accused Daniel of being rebellious against King Nebuchadnezzar. Satan accused David of committing unforgivable sins when he committed adultery with Bathsheba and caused the death of her husband Uriah. Satan accused Job of being a hypocrite and committing evil. Satan accused Jesus' own disciple, Simon Peter, when he denied Jesus. All these accusations were intended to make these people quit and lose hope. However, these accusative situations ended by only making these people seek God and become stronger later on. One of Satan's weapons is accusation to try to cause guilt and shame. Satan accuses you to make you believe that your pain is going to drive you to despair. Your hardships and trials are not shame. The Bible says, "Do not be afraid; you will not be put to shame. Do not fear disgrace; you will not be humiliated (Isa 54:4)." God can use afflictions and hardships to draw you to Him to welcome your victory.

If you feel guilt, this is not the same as shame, but guilt can be a sign of the conviction of the Holy Spirit to remind you that God provides a forgiveness through the blood of His Son, Jesus, if you come to Him. God said, "For I will forgive their iniquities and will remember their sins no more (Heb 8:12 BLB)." Satan is trying to use your guilt and make you think that God accuses you to make you feel guilty and to drive you to despair. God does not intend for you to live with guilt feelings. Do not let your feelings determine God. Rather, let God determine your feelings. Life in Christ is not life in fear. God is not the author of fear. It is the work of devil to put fear and doubt in your mind, so that you will not believe God for your second chance. Do not allow fear to take charge. You are not a slave to fear; rather, you are a child of God. Get rid of that kind of accusation, and together with David say to yourself his powerful proclamation: "I sought the LORD, and he answered me; he delivered me from all my fears (Ps 34:4)." David had faith instead of fear. Therefore, he was determined to seek the Lord and to be delivered from fears.

Like Joseph, Daniel, and David, Job went through a painful life. Job, however, experienced not only the afflictions of loss and disease, but the accusations of his close friends. Influenced by Satan, the three friends of Job were very eager to blame Job. The only thing that Satan would like to see in your life is to see you battered, and the only thing he hates is to see you better. Satan does not like to see you progress and improve; rather, he likes to see you stagnant and diminished. Your failure is Satan's success, and he will continue to keep you from your success. The only assignment that the devil has is to destroy you so that you will accept your lot and never bounce back—ever. Satan's ambition is to attack your mind with his lies. However, God's affection is greater than the devil's ambition. Therefore, you are not finished yet, no matter how hard the devil has pressed you. Have an attitude of resiliency.

Paul expressed it in these words: "We are hard pressed on every side, but not crushed; perplexed, but not in despair; persecuted, but not abandoned; struck down, but not destroyed. We always carry around in our body the death of Jesus, so that the life of Jesus may also be revealed in our body" (2 Cor 4:8-10). This is your battle, and you are not going to lose it. Jesus already won the battle for you! Your pain and suffering will not end on the battlefield, because God is there for you and with you.

Deliver Us From Evil

Jesus, the Son of God, was aware of the work of Satan, and Jesus went through the devil's temptations. In His humanity, Jesus experienced these. Right after He was filled with the Holy Spirit, the devil was ready to confront Jesus in the wilderness (Luke 4:1-2). Jesus understood every inch of the wilderness. He had been through the wilderness, the worst of all the personal wilderness that existed and would ever exist. Satan dared to come up against the Son of Almighty God. However, in the face of temptation, Jesus Christ used the means that is available to believers in order to resist temptation: the word of God.

The word of God is the most powerful weapon that you have to defeat the work of the devil in your life. You cannot fight the devil in your own strength, nor can you become afraid of him. Rather, you can use the word of God appropriately against the forces of evil. Confronted by the devil, Jesus fought back using the word of God. Every time the devil confronted Jesus, He said, "It is written *and* forever remains written, 'YOU SHALL NOT TEST THE LORD YOUR GOD (Matt 4:7 AMP).'"

Whenever the devil is trying to attack your mind in order to deny you your victory, then take the time to pray in the Spirit, as well as to take up the shield of faith, with which you can extinguish all the flaming arrows of the evil one, and take the helmet of salvation and the sword of the Spirit, which is the word of God, to protect yourself from the enemy (Eph 6:16-18).

In His humanity, Jesus was not immune to the schemes of Satan. Neither are we. Jesus knew that Judas was influenced by Satan to betray Him (Luke 22:3, 21). Jesus saw Peter used by Satan. Knowing that He would suffer and be killed at the hands of the elders, chief priests, and scribes, Peter was trying to defend Jesus. However, Jesus turned and said to Peter, "Get behind Me, Satan! You are a stumbling block to me (Matt 16:23)." Jesus knew that Peter was trying to defend Him, but Jesus also knew that the will of the Father was for Him to suffer, and Jesus was fulfilling God's plan through the pain and suffering. Peter wanted Jesus to gain His crown as the prince of the world, but Jesus knew that to gain the crown, He had to go to the cross. Jesus rebuked Satan, who had influenced the mind of Peter, and Satan was addressed in the same terms as those that had been spoken to Satan in the wilderness (Matt 4:10).

We are involved in a spiritual war against evil. One night, in the first hospital in the city where the airplane accident took place, I was confronted by Satan. My wife was planning to transfer me to the second hospital. Preparations had been made to fly me on the next morning. Suddenly, though, my temperature went so high for the whole night that my body became dehydrated due to vast amounts of fluid being excreted from the burns. I was getting weaker and weaker, and I looked pale. I felt as though my whole body was drenched and stuck down (as though multiple ropes were tying down my body). I complained about this to my wife. She replied, "There aren't any ropes tying you down." Bent in prayer, she prayed and cried at my bedside, and then with a harsh voice she rebuked Satan. Suddenly I felt all the rope fall away, and my temperature went back to normal.

This spiritual warfare was described as a war of faith which lasts until we enter eternal life (2 Tim 4:7-8). However, the victory of the believer has been obtained by Christ Himself through His death on the cross. Jesus launched the successful attack on Satan, and Jesus disarmed the power and rule of evil (Matt 12:29; Luke 10:18; John 12:31).

Of course, not all pain and trials are caused by Satan. Sometimes God may allow these for your good, whereas Satan only does this for your bad. The pain and suffering of Jesus brought us life and hope, but the pain and suffering brought by Satan causes hopelessness. In His faithfulness to bear the suffering, Jesus wants us to be faithful and identify with Him, but Satan wants us to believe in his lies. Of course, you do not deny pain as though it never happened. Rather, you face it by faith. Ask God to give you a strong shoulder to carry it, and in His time, He will lift it off to allow you to celebrate your victory graduation. Satan, on the other hand, wants to keep you from your graduation. He wants you to stay in your present pain level, unmoved and not knowing what to do—whereas God wants you to experience progress every day. God loves to see you move to another level daily, but He also acknowledges the power of Satan who holds you and pulls you down. Satan never takes his eyes off God's children. Therefore, when Jesus' disciples asked Him how they should pray to God, the Father, Jesus taught them a simple, but powerful, prayer:

"This, then, is how you should pray:
'Our Father in heaven,
hallowed be your name,
your kingdom come,
your will be done,
on earth as it is in heaven.
Give us today our daily bread.
And forgive us our debts,
as we also have forgiven our debtors.
And lead us not into temptation,
but deliver us from the evil one.'" (Matt 6:9-13)

Leading into this, Jesus told His disciples that, " . . . Your Father knows what you need (Matt 6:8)." He knows that we need His provision, but He also wants us not to be defeated by the evil one. There are six requests in this prayer: the first three relate to God's holiness and will. The remaining three relate to our daily needs. In all these needs, God wants His purpose manifested in our daily lives. He wants us to be victorious believers every day, but He also acknowledges that the devil wants to steal our victory. Therefore, He teaches us to pray: "And lead us not into temptation but deliver us from the evil one." All believers are special targets of satanic hostility, and he means to do evil. Therefore, we must never forget to pray so that we are freed from his power and evil plan. Just as with other provisions, deliverance from the snares of Satan is our daily bread and provision. This provision is freedom from the accuser. Satan accuses you so that pain will never leave you. Do not take that evil thought. Rather, replace it with the promise of God. God gives you His Spirit to overcome that fear. "For God did not give us a spirit of timidity, but a spirit of power, of love and of self-discipline (2 Tim 1:7)." Jesus says, "If the Son makes you free, you shall be free indeed (John 8:36)." Enjoy His total freedom in you. No one can take it from you.

God Made It for Good

The devil is a liar. He wants you to believe that you will never get away from your pain. However, God wants you to know that you will get through it. The devil wants to tell you that your storm will destroy you. However, God wants to tell you that some of the storm will clear your path. God wants to assure you that your pain is not a setback, but it is God's setup. Many people have experienced the cunning schemes of the devil, and some of those people became victims of the devil's setup. They could not really see it from God's perspective.

Lying for many months in bed waiting for healing was truly painful for me. In my low points, the devil took the opportunity to confront me with these accusations: "Flying in the airplane that morning was a big mistake." "Recovering from severe burn wounds is not easy." "Your scars will make you look ugly." "You will be disabled for the rest of your life." These were all the cunning schemes of the devil to make me feel bad for myself. I must admit that I was terrorized by these accusations.

I am not trying to give credit to Satan, but Satan's power is real. I was taunted and oppressed. Nevertheless, we have a source of power which is much more powerful than the power of Satan: the person of the Lord Jesus Christ. My wife and I called on the name of Jesus to bind Satan's lies and to set loose the oppression. Slowly, Christ's peace invaded my heart. Satan failed to victimize me. What a powerful and beautiful name is Jesus! What a privilege God gives us in the authority to overcome the schemes of Satan—and in Christ, we are even more than overcomers (Rom 8:37). The Gospel tells us that, " . . . Whatever you bind on earth will be bound in heaven, and whatever you loose on earth will be loosed in heaven (Matt 18:18)." Your trials and pain are not going to make you look bad. This is only an intimidation of Satan. God gives you an authority, and you must use this authority in the name of Jesus to receive your healing and deliverance. Isaiah 54:14-15,17 gives us a wonderful promise from God:

> Tyranny will be far from you; you will have nothing to fear. Terror will be far removed; it will not come near you. If anyone does attack you, it will not be my doing; whoever attacks you will surrender to you. . . . no weapon forged against you will prevail, and you will refute every tongue that accuses you.

Here God comforts Israel, who was suffering, by describing the peace, victory, and glory of the restored Israel, after the fear and terror of the enemies. These words comfort you who are experiencing severe hardship or trials. In fact, in times of suffering, God's continued presence with us is the greatest source of comfort that He can provide for us (Ps 46:7,11; 91:15). When we are pressured by temptation and shaken by the stormy state of life, we must remember that it is precisely this situation that causes God to be merciful to us and to approach us so that we can be strong again. The devil says that you cannot make it, but his power is too weak to keep you from making it. In fact, the power of God is strong enough to keep you from falling.

The wicked plan of Joseph's brothers was not enough to end Joseph's dream by putting him in the pit. The dreamer, a cynical name for Joseph, was triggered by jealousy, and this jealousy grew to hatred, and hatred resulted in wanting to destroy Joseph's life. The devil was using his family. Joseph was treated badly by his own brothers. However, his brothers' evil act to destroy his life turned out to strengthen Joseph. Regardless of what Joseph went through as a result of his brothers' wicked scheme, at the end of this part of Joseph's story, he was able to say to all his brothers, "Don't be afraid. Am I in the place of God? You intended to harm me, but God intended it for good to accomplish what is now being done, the saving of many lives (Gen 50:20)."

Implied from Joseph's words, he was basically saying, "If I had not gone through these hardships and trials, I would not have enjoyed success, and I would not be able to help you and so many others." Indeed, if Joseph had not been put in the pit, he would not have arrived in the palace. Joseph held on to his pit experience, and he was able to receive his graduation from the school of hardship. Ultimately, Joseph realized that his pit was only temporary. The wicked brothers made the pit as a chain to bind Joseph, but God designed it for a chance to bounce back. The brothers planned the pit to break Joseph down, but God used it for a new breakthrough. Joseph's brothers intended the pit to harm him, but God intended it for his good. Indeed, what was meant for evil, God meant for good.

There is about to be a shift in your life. Get ready for your next breakthrough. You have been through enough, and a breakthrough is on the way. Be ready for the brand-new life breakthrough. God is not through with you yet. There are many times when God allowed tribulation and calamity as a punishment, for example as he did at Sodom and Gomorrah (Gen 19). However, in most situations, things turn out better when we hold on to God and allow Him to take over the pit situations. God is engineering your pit for some greater purposes that will take you to your palace. Many times, we refuse to withstand in the pit. Instead, we have a slow decent into the depths of despair and depression. Like Joseph, the only thing that you must do is remember that your God, who gave you a dream, is coming to help pull you out of the pit. God is with you in both the pit and the palace, and God promises to make something good out of the pit that caused devastation and depression in your life (Rom 8:28). Satan's proclamation is, "It's over." However, God's reconciliation is over you, and

He is not done with you yet. God is turning your wailing into dancing, removing your sackcloth, and clothing you with joy (Ps 30:11).

Having been in a low point and intimidated by King Saul, David did not allow himself to stay in a devastated mood. He knew that God is a faithful God. David convinces us that God was able to turn David's sorrow into joy, as he said, "His anger lasts only a moment, his goodness for a lifetime. Tears may flow in the night, but joy comes in the morning (Ps 30:5 GNT)." David knew that the darkest hour meant that dawn is just in sight and hope still walks with the broken.

Things are about to turn around, and God is arranging it in our favor. Therefore, He is willing to fight our battles. Never forget that God is with you in good times and in bad times, on the mountain top and in the valleys, in joy and tears, in blessings and trials, for better and for worse. Whatever you are going through, God is right there with you. He is there in every season that you walk through. God's grace and mercy drive you back to Him to enjoy your second chance in life. This is your chance to make it come to pass for the better.

Chapter 7

YOU CAN BE WHOLE AGAIN

*"The LORD is close to the brokenhearted and saves those
who are crushed in spirit" (Psalm 34:18) "He heals
the brokenhearted and binds up their wounds"
(Psalm 147:3.)*

Pain and brokenness can bring feelings of numbness,
emptiness, and depression. These can lead to loss of
hope and loss of passion for life, which ultimately could
resort to ending lives. This can happen to anyone, regardless
how of spiritual they seem to be. Your numbness, emptiness,
and depression are the soft targets for the thief. We read in
John 10:10 that, "The thief comes only to steal and kill and
destroy." The thief will tell you that you will never be healed
again. Let me remind you that when somebody tells you that,
"You will not be healed," then warn them that this is the
voice of Satan. You are not destined to be in pain. God did
not create you to be the victim of pain. You are destined to
reign over sickness and pain. God will turn around every area

of your hurt. Therefore, God promises to restore whatever the thief has stolen from you. In fact, God not only restores, but He is more than able to multiply what has been stolen by the enemy. Indeed, "God works for the good of those who love him (Rom 8:28)." God has His own way to restore and to beautify for our good.

When something is broken, the world normally discards it, because they think that it is difficult or useless to try to put it together again. In Japanese tradition, there is a technique that is used to fix broken pottery that is called *kintsugi*. It uses a precious metal—liquid gold, liquid silver or lacquer dusted with powdered gold—to bring together the pieces of a broken pottery item and at the same time enhance the breaks. The technique consists in joining fragments and giving them a new, more refined aspect, and the pottery now becomes beautiful piece of art.[1]

This technique makes the point that the breaks can become more precious. Likewise, if your life is full of pain and brokenness, then the hand of the Potter is more than able to fix and heal it totally. Jesus is the potter and we are the clay. If you surrender your brokenness to the potter's hand, then He will make something beautiful out of your brokenness. The pain will end, and the door of healing will open. The enemy wants you to lose hope in order to make a season of miracles cease. A miracle is on the horizon and you must be ready for it. God keeps His promises and, therefore, the promise of healing is on the way. When Job was tested with misery and suffering, he experienced deep sorrow and anger, and he questioned God, all of which were caused by what seemed to be unjust misery (Job 19:6-7; 27:1; 31:35). However, God loved Job. Job's condition was restored, and he received double restitution. Job said that God does everything well. Everything that God permits to happen is carried out in wisdom and with a purpose. At the end of the narrative, Job finally witnessed and experienced the goodness of God, and Job expressed this in his own words, "My ears had heard of you but now my eyes have seen you (Job 42:5)."

At the beginning of the book of Job, we learn that God gave Satan permission to have power over all of Job's possessions, and the devil immediately carried out his plan. The purpose of the devil was to make Job blaspheme God and to leave his godly life. It was in one day that Job received news from various places that his cattle and donkeys were taken and many servants were killed by the Sabeans. The sheep and other servants were burned by fire from the sky. The camels were taken and more servants were killed by the Chaldeans. All of Job's children were killed in a storm. Satan destroyed everything of Job's in just one day. The text describes a barrage of doom from one disaster to another disaster. All that Job had was now vanished. His children were gone, his possessions were gone, and most of his servants were gone. Job was deeply grieved. He tore his robe and shaved his head, like people used to do at a time of grieving.

However, Job's sorrow was not over with these losses. In Job 2, the devil came at him with further damage. Job was plagued by the devil with painful boils from the soles of his feet to the top of his head. Job's entire body was covered with boils. His supposedly dear wife mocked him, instead of comforting him. Job, who once was rich and healthy, was now a very poor and a sick person who was despised by his wife. Job used to enjoy his comfortable life. Now his body became like dust and ashes (Job 30:19 KJV). He used to be served by many servants. Now he only had a pottery shard to scratch his wound. He used to smell so good. Now he smelled of wounds. These changes were very drastic and extraordinary. Job's family, wealth, and health were finished. Job now lived a life full of suffering. Job's suffering was deepened when his wife also insulted his loyalty to God and told him to, " . . . Curse God and die!" (Job 2:9).

Through all pain and suffering, the Scripture explains that Job did not sin in what he said (Job 2:10). Job's suffering was not directly connected to anything that he had done wrong, but he allowed himself to be tested by God through adversity. Job did not rebel against God in his heart. Rather, he trusted and was faithful to God. No wonder in the final chapter of the book of Job, God restored everything double: ". . . The LORD restored his fortunes and gave him twice as much as he had before (Job 42:10)." Job passed the test and showed us an amazing example. Furthermore, at the end of the narrative, Job had more possessions and children, and Job lived a long and blessed life.

Having read of Job's suffering, you might say, "I could never handle the things that Job faced! In fact, I can't handle suffering at all." Do not worry. Make a decision not to worry today. Trust God to lead you one day at a time. You may concern about your pain but do not turn it into illegitimate worry, it will drain your energy. You cannot add a single hour to your life by worrying (Matt 6:27). Corrie ten Boom, a Nazi concentration camp survivor and an exemplar of Christian faith in action, said, "Worry does not empty tomorrow of sorrow; it empties today of strength."[2]

God knows what you have been through. God will give you what you need when you need it: not before, never after, but when you need it. God never steals anything from you. Rather, He wants to return what the devil has stolen. The devil comes only to cause destruction, but God brings full restoration. He makes everything better than before. When I needed healing from the severe burns, He gave this to me in His time. I really am grateful to have been allowed to go through this painful experience because the incident made me whole—not only physically, but also in spirit and soul. God is never bound to our time. He is only bound to His time and His promises. God's promise is to make us holy and whole (1 Thess 5:23)

True believers must prepare themselves to be tested by God through adversity, and they must also be ready to receive good things from God's hands. When hardship comes, a believer who does not feel any sin or rebellion against God in his heart must surrender his soul to God. Faith in God as a loving God in the midst of trials and oppression will reveal the complete victory of faith. Creflo Dollar once said, "If we are to experience this supernatural restoration, however, we must have faith that it will happen. King David, who suffered much adversity, confessed that he would have fainted and given up if he had not believed he would see God's goodness. Refusing to fear, and instead rejoicing and being glad when nothing is going right, opens the door to allow God to do great things and restore to us all the lost years."[3] If you have experienced a loss today—your possessions or your health—do not be discouraged, but wait patiently. It is about time. God will restore and multiply back to you. God is going to give back to you what Satan took from you.

He is the God that Heals Us

God's favor will change your life for you to be a better person. However, pain can also change your attitude—causing you to become a bitter person. Therefore, allow yourself to be surrounded by God's grace so that pain will not have any chance to change you into bitterness. You may not have experienced a complete healing yet, or you may still be struggling right now, but God's grace is sufficient for you (2 Cor 12:9). There is grace for every pain and suffering that you endure. Therefore, do not listen to voice of the devil, but rather, listen to the voice of grace. Listening to the voice of the devil only makes you regretful and bitter. However, listening to the voice of God will make you whole again. The voice of Satan is a disgrace to human beings. However, the voice of God is a grace for us. Therefore, the Bible says, "If you will diligently listen *and* pay attention to the voice of the LORD your God, and do what is right in His sight, and listen to His commandments, and keep [foremost in your thoughts and actively obey] all His precepts *and* statutes, then I will not put on you any of the diseases which I have put on the Egyptians; for I am the LORD who heals you(Exod 15:26 AMP)."

There is a reason God says, "I am the LORD who heals you." He has the power to heal. He overcomes diseases. He is willing to heal. Above all, He is not only good at making promises but also good at keeping promises. Do not listen to the voice that says that you never will be whole again. Listen to the I Am who promises to heal you and to make you whole again. The God whom we trust did promise this. It is not a promise made by human beings but made by your Creator. Jeremiah, a prophet of God, confirmed this and said, "'I will restore you to heath and heal your wounds,' declares the LORD, 'because you are called an outcast, Zion for whom no one cares (Jer 30:17).'"

One thing that God cannot and will not do is to lie. God promised to Himself that He would heal Zion, whom He cared for. He makes a promise to Himself, and He does it for His name's sake. He does not make and keep promises so that you can feel good, but so that you can have His proof that He is good to you. In Deuteronomy 6:4, God says to Israel that, "The LORD our God, the LORD is one." Indeed, "There can be but one eternal, one omnipotent, one omnipresent, one infinite, one that is originally and of himself good."[4] God's goodness is running after your sadness, sickness, and pain, and He is working in it. Indeed, God the Healer is still working among His people and He wants to heal them.

Infected by Coronavirus Disease, the family took me to the Emergency Room three times due to high fever and unusual tightness in my chest. Following three days with the virus, my wife and my two sons were diagnosed with COVID-19 and tested positive. We all had what came to be known in my house as "the plague". Oh, it was scary knowing the news story filled with ventilators and ultimate death. The power of the invisible enemy suddenly attacked us, but it cannot kill us because the power of the blood of Jesus is greater than the power of the pandemic diseases. Just as Jesus healed me and gave the second chance to live and survived the airplane crash, this time He also healed me and my family from the coronavirus disease and protected us from the fatal attack of COVID-19.

The Bible speaks of healing through the work of Jesus Christ and through faith in God. Healing is a by-product of Jesus' stripes that He endured before going to the cross. The Bible says, "But He was wounded for our transgressions, He was bruised for our iniquities; the chastisement for our peace was upon Him, and by His stripes we are healed" (Isa 53:5 NKJV). Jesus . . ."Himself took our infirmities and bore our sicknesses (Matt 8:17 NKJV)." Peter says that Jesus . . ."Himself bore our sins in His own body on the tree, that we, having died to sins, might live for righteousness—by whose stripes you were healed (1 Pet 2:24 NKJV)."

Believers in the early church experienced miracles of healing. Believers continue to experience these today, and these will be experienced in the future. Divine healing is still taking place, and you can experience it today. The miracle-working power of God is still at work today because Jesus Christ is the same yesterday and today and forever (Heb

13:8). Some people are trying to create doubt in you by twisting and doubting the miracle-working power of God. The psalmist confirms that God heals all our diseases (Ps 103:3). God does not lie. This is a present-tense promise, and it is applicable today. The message of God for you is still the same—God heals yesterday, today, and tomorrow.

Healing is provided for all in the atonement through the finished work of Christ Jesus, and this healing points back to the time when the work of Christ was accomplished on the cross. God has overcome our sicknesses and infirmities at the cross, and it was done. God is saying to you to rest in Him because He is already at work. With the juridical action of Christ in atonement, merit was made available to us. The work of Jesus was perfect, complete, and final, and therefore, healing was accomplished. God wants us to experience His provision. God wants us to be in good health and for all to go well with us, even as our souls are getting along well (3 John 2). God creates our healthy bodies for His dwelling place. God wants His people to be healthy, accompanied by His blessings.

Jesus Wants Us Healed Wholly

Jesus comes to heal, not to punish. Abraham's descendants traveled to Egypt, and over the course of time, they were enslaved by the Egyptians. Exodus 2:23–5 relates what happened: "The Israelites groaned under their slavery and cried out. Out of the slavery their cry for help rose up to God. God heard their groaning, and God remembered God's covenant with Abraham" (NRSVA) God's blessing to all people was fulfilled in the coming of Jesus, the Messiah, a descendant of Abraham, through whom people are blessed spiritually and physically.

During His ministry, Jesus told His disciples that His coming to the world was to bring the Kingdom of God, which brings life and not death (John 10:10). "Jesus traveled throughout the region of Galilee, teaching in the synagogues, announcing the good news of the Kingdom, and healing every kind of disease and illness (Matt 4:23). "Jesus healed people out of compassion for their [pain and] suffering. But His acts of healing were also dramatic signs that the Kingdom of God had indeed drawn near. Jesus was proclaiming that God's power was present in a new way. His healings proved the point."[5]

Jesus not only demonstrated the Kingdom of God as a reality by Himself, but He also sent His disciples "to preach the Kingdom of God, the gospel, which gives an account of the kingdom of the Messiah," including, " . . . His kingly office and power (Luke 9:2)."[6] One way in which He manifested His deity and power was in healing. This Kingdom is not a political kingdom, but it is a divine healing Kingdom as He promised to Israel (Exod 15:26). Jesus has compassion for every person who suffers with disease and pain.

Jesus also has compassion for a broken body (Matt 8:16). God is able and willing to restore our physical bodies, and many types of physical diseases have been happening. We are created in the image of God (Gen 1:27). Not only did God create us with physical bodies, He personally was incarnated with a physical body. He healed physical bodies, He was resurrected with a physical body, and He gave the gift of healing physical bodies to His church. God's compassion gripped us in order for us to experience His healing. I experienced a complete healing of burns on fifty percent of my body years ago from an airplane accident, and now I have gone back to my normal life after I received my physical healing. It is His desire for His people to be healed. Indeed, Jesus has compassion for us to be healed from broken bodies and broken hearts.

God also has compassion for a broken heart (Ps 147:3). Jesus binds up the broken hearted. David the psalmist said that, "The LORD is close to the brokenhearted and saves those who are crushed in spirit (Ps 34:18)." He who made the heart has power to heal the heart, and He is willing to heal the heart. Jesus has compassion for a broken life (John 8:1-11). If the religious people came to condemn adultery, then Jesus, on the other hand, came to forgive and to restore the adulterer.

God speaks about wholeness in three dimensions, which are body, soul, and spirit, but these components of human beings are not precisely separate categories. John Wesley, founder of Methodism, spoke about holistic health during his ministry. "Through his sermons and writings, he often advocated a holistic approach towards spiritual and physical health." In a letter written in 1778 to Alexander Knox, a theological writer, Wesley wrote, "It will be a double blessing if you give yourself up to the Great Physician, that He may heal soul and body together. And unquestionably this is His design. He wants to give you . . . both inward and outward health.'[7]

Televangelist Oral Roberts, the founder of Oral Roberts University and a former chronic tuberculosis sufferer, affirms that healing begins in the inner man. He says that one's soul governs this mortal life and passes on to the body and mind its illness, distress, and torment. Roberts says, "In the Bible, healing is for the whole man. It's for the body, it's for the soul, it's for the mind, for finances. It's for any problem that needs to be healed."[8] Healing is being claimed as an integral element of proclaiming the good news of salvation. Jesus healed the paralyzed man both body and soul (Mark 2:10). Forgiveness and healing represent the holistic healing power of soul-salvation.

During my plane accident, I saw the body of the aircraft that I was on shattered and burned into ashes. Fifty percent of my body was burned with first to third degree burns. I went through pain, suffering, and desperate moments. However, I experienced a divine moment with God when I enjoyed God's presence as never before, and through it all I came out victoriously. God not only healed my body, but He restored my soul. God helped me pass through it. Jesus rescued me and gave me a new life with a new heart to the point of making a commitment to love Him more and to be willing to serve Him, as a response to His wholeness and healing that I received from my Healer.

My healing was real, and I am the living testimony of it. The New Testament recorded many miracles performed by Jesus. The book of John recorded seven miracles done by Jesus. Some of them were miraculous healings, and all of them are real. The healing of the official's dying son in John 4:43-54 was real. The healing of the crippled man at the pool of Bethesda in John 5:1-9 was true. The recovery of the man born blind in John 9:1-41 was factual. Even the raising of Lazarus from the dead in John 11:1-44 was recorded as a true narrative. One real healing that is recorded in the book of Matthew is the narrative of the woman with the issue of blood. She walked into the crowd to find Jesus, and said to herself, "If I can but touch the Hem of His garment, I shall be whole (Matt 9:21-22 KJV)." She believed in Jesus to heal her.

The story healing of the woman is so inspirational and unique. It shows us that the woman lived her faith and was determined to encounter Jesus. The woman positioned herself for her healing and participated in her healing. Her actions speaks of her faith in Jesus. She entrusted her condition to Jesus and the power of Jesus through His garment to heal her. Jesus fulfills His promise to those who believe in His name. Furthermore, in many cases, Jesus spoke to or touched the sick people for healing, but this time the woman touched Jesus instead. She moved beyond the reality of her weak physical condition and invoked her faith. Her believing faith moved the heart of Jesus, and the presence of the Holy Spirit invaded her life and brought her healing. God's presence was embodied in her life in the form of healing. God is present in our lives in the form of total healing: physically, emotionally, and spiritually.

For human beings, disease or brokenness may be a problem—but for God, disease is not a problem, because God is able and willing to make you whole. It becomes a problem for us if we do not have faith in Him. Therefore, all you can do is reach out and touch Him by faith. All you can do is reach out and touch Him in faith. There is more healing available in the hem of Jesus's garment than in a hospital or drug store. It is Christ Jesus' will that everyone gets healed in every area of their lives. Therefore, the Scripture says, "Beloved, I pray that you may prosper in all things and be in health, just as your soul prospers (3 John 1:2 NKJV)." Jesus takes our weakness, sorrow, sickness, and pain, and He makes us whole again.

Chapter 8

MAKE YOUR TEST BECOME
YOUR TESTIMONY

*"Your testimonies are my heritage forever, for
they are the joy of my heart. I incline my heart to
perform your statutes forever, to the end."*
(Psalm 119:111-112 ESV)

*"Blessed is the one who perseveres under trial because,
having stood the test, that person will receive the crown of
life that the Lord has promised to those who love him"*
(James 1:12)

L ife is not playing in the playground but fighting in the
battleground. The claims that life is good and God is
good only remain theories until they are tested. A test is not
intended to fail you, but to reveal who you are. In the test,
there are two voices that claim your victory—a voice of God
and a voice of Satan. In the test, there are always two voices
to yell at you. One voice will pronounce your victory, and the

other voice will denounce your victory. One voice says, "Well done, you are a champion," and the other voice says, "Poor you, you are a loser." The voice of a champion lifts you up, but the voice of a loser pulls you down. These two voices feed your mind and influence your actions.

Making choices is not easy. Therefore, we call this a battleground. But do not worry, because you are not alone in the battle: God is watching your fight, and He is ready to take over on your behalf. Perhaps Satan is whispering in your ear that you are going to fail and are totally defeated in this pain. Satan brings fiery darts to penetrate and destroy your mind, but when you have on the helmet of hope, his whispers cannot penetrate and destroy your mind. The helmet of hope and the word of God are your protection.

Moses assured the Israelites concerning their fear of the Egyptian army that was chasing them, saying, "The LORD will fight for you; you need only to be still (Exod 14:14)." Moses only asked the Israelites to be still so that they could hear the voice of God, and not the noise of their oppressors. Do not listen to the whispers of Satan. Do not make Satan happy. This is a time to fight back You are a mighty warrior of God. A warrior is trained to listen to the voice of God to make a move. Lisa Bevere says, "There is an invitation to revere God, to be still and to know. Know what? Know Him as God by allowing Him to reveal Himself in the midst of your pain, conflict, or crisis. He wants to be the final word you hear before sleep overtakes you."[1]

A test is meant to show whose voice you listen to. Make a choice of faith concerning whose voice you listen to. The more you have faith in God, the easier it is for you to hear God's voice. The more you have faith, the easier it is for you to pass the hardest test. When I was in a dying state in a hospital after my airplane crash, I was experiencing a unique encounter. While the nurses were dressing me on a Friday afternoon, suddenly my temperature rose very high. I was shivering, I felt very heavy in my chest, and suddenly I could not breathe. My wife said that all the nurses were panicked and were calling the doctor, but they could not contact the doctor. The nurses tried to help me breathe, but I could not. They put oxygen in me, but it did not help either. I was on death's doorstep. My wife said that I was gone for fifteen minutes. I did not feel pain anymore. I was ready to go home on that Friday afternoon.

Suddenly, I saw myself lying in a long dark tunnel, my body was wrapped with white cloth, and I heard a voice saying, "Say goodbye, say goodbye, . . ." But suddenly, I heard another voice saying, "Hold on, hold on, . . ." These two voices were fighting for me. I may interpret that the first voice was the voice of Satan trying to take my life, and the second voice was the voice of angels upholding me. Then suddenly from the other end of the long dark tunnel, a light came toward me and became bigger and bigger, and out of the light I heard a voice calling, "Daddy, Daddy, . . ." It was my youngest son, Jonathan, one and a half years old, and he was running toward me in the long dark tunnel. Suddenly, I could remember that I have children and family, and my wife said that she saw my mouth move slowly. I had miraculously regained consciousness and my breathing ability. My time was not up yet. I praise God for giving me a second chance to live.

You see, there are two powers in the testing time: power to pull you down to confuse your victory, and power to lift you up to confirm your victory. God will lift you up out of the pit. Your victory is always on the other side of your pain. Your life will be ended in the great end of the tunnel. In my dying state, I heard a gentle voice, yet so powerful, in the long dark tunnel, confirming my victory over death. I passed the test, and it became my testimony to many people all over the world. I thank God for giving me a second chance to live. Through this recounting, I long to witness the love of God which I received.

Do you remember when God asked Abraham to sacrifice his only legitimate son, Isaac, that he had been awaiting for so long? Abraham had been waiting for Isaac to be born for twenty-five years since God made the promise. Waiting for such a long time was a sacrifice. Waiting for your healing, your recovery, and your breakthrough is not easy. It needs you to sacrifice: your time, your money, and even your emotions. However, God may want more of a sacrifice to see the real you in order to perfect His plan in you. Waiting for Isaac to be born for twenty-five years, and Sarah conceiving and giving birth in old age, was a hard enough time for Abraham and Sarah.

However, God wanted to see Abraham sacrifice more to God in order to test Abraham's heart. God asked Abraham to sacrifice Isaac for Him, and God asked Abraham to slay Isaac on the Mount Moriah. Abraham took Isaac to the mountain ready to slay him as a sacrifice to God. When Abraham was about to kill Isaac, suddenly God sent His angel to tell Abraham: Stop! Don't kill Isaac. This is just a test. Abraham saw a ram in the bush. God gave him a ram to sacrifice instead of his son (Gen 22:1-14). Abraham passed his test, and then God swore by Himself to Abraham: "I will surely bless you and make your descendants as numerous as the stars in the sky and as the sand on the seashore. Your descendants will take possession of the cities of their enemies, and through your offspring all nations on earth will be blessed, because you have obeyed me (Gen 22:17-18)." Abraham's obedience was worth his victory, and in this test, he became an example to his descendants as a man of faith. Abraham's faith did not waver in the test, and the Scripture use this as a testimony to the world.

Perhaps you have been waiting for your test to become your testimony for a very long time, and while you have been waiting, you are still going through many pains that make you almost give up and feel hopeless. God made a promise to Abraham that God was with him during Abraham's tough test, and God did it. God has promised us that as our days, so will our strength be (Deut 33:25). Your life is not horrible, and God is preparing you for something incredible. He has promised us that if He has begun a good work in us, He will complete it, and He will take care of accomplishing what He has said (Phil 1:6). You read in the Bible the amazing example of Job, who passed the test after going through a real test of faith. Job could have chosen to remain sick and to feel bitterness towards his wife who despised him, his three friends who mocked him, and God who allowed him to go through it all. However, Job chose to remain faithful in that testing, and he came out victoriously.

What Job went through was a true experience in real life. Just reading about Job's afflictions and hardships is troubling already to us, let alone experiencing these. However, do not let your heart be troubled. Through it all, God's eyes were never off Job. God continued to follow and monitor Job during his tests: from his first test, the loss of his property and children, to his second test, the loss of his health. God was still on Job's side.

Satan may have stricken Job with many afflictions, but Satan only did so within the boundaries set by God. Satan could only take Job to the end of his rope, but not to end his life. Job's pain and suffering started with grief, but these ended with happiness and relief. Job's pain only gave him a test, but his victory gave him a testimony. Job passed the test, and he announced it as a great spiritual victory to the people around him. "Then all his brothers, all his sisters, and all those who had been his acquaintances before, came to him and ate food with him in his house . . . Now the Lord blessed the latter *days* of Job more than his beginning (Job 42:11-12 NKJV)." Job celebrated the goodness and faithfulness of God, and he made it a testimony to his family and friends.

God assures you that He, " . . . Is faithful; he will not let you be tempted beyond what you can bear. But when you are tempted, he will also provide a way out so that you can endure it (1 Cor 10:13)." God never lets you suffer without a purpose, even if you do not understand the reasons. Job passed the test, and he gave us an amazing example of how to make the test into a testimony, because Job remained faithful to God in the midst of the trials and tribulations of life.

The Test Makes Us Better

In times of sorrow and pain, it is hard to say, "I am better." When emotions are raw, it is difficult to see light beyond the darkness. Darkness soaks up life and keeps us from seeing a glimpse of hope ahead. In times of blazing pain, we have a tendency to turn our backs and to blame someone or God. Some people cannot hold on, and they choose to run away from God and become bitter. Allowing yourself to be bitter can make everything worse, and it will ruin your future. Bitterness causes hopelessness, but joyousness will enable you to see what lies ahead. There is no optimism in the lives of hopeless people. Bitterness brings out pessimism and makes your life paralyzed. A paralyzed person cannot make a move. This can be dangerous, and it can create a point of no return. There is no progress to be made when you hold back from your past.

The story of the paralyzed man who had been an invalid for thirty-eight years is an example of a point of no return. However, the compassion of Jesus made him well (John 5:1-14). The man had been waiting for his turn to be healed in the Pool of Bethesda for such a long time, but he failed many times. Many people had been healed in the water that was stirred by the angels. However, the paralyzed man always missed his turn to get into the water, because he depended on other people's help to take him to the water. Nevertheless, when Jesus came, finally the man was healed. In His mercy, Jesus was pleased to help him.

Have you been paralyzed by your pain and felt defeated? How long have you been paralyzed? Do not look at what Satan did. It does not matter how long you have been paralyzed. It is not about your pain. It is about your willingness to present your case to Jesus by faith. Jesus saw the invalid man lying there, and Jesus learned that the man had been in this condition for a long time (John 5:5). Paralysis will come to an end, and you are the next one. Don't miss it! Jesus is asking you, "Do you want Me to heal you?" This is a sign that breakthrough is around the corner. You can be better, because in a moment you will hear Jesus say, "Stand up, you will be walking again."

In Lamentations 3:19-22, Jeremiah reminds us that in the midst of suffering, we need to hold onto hope: "I remember my affliction and my wandering, the bitterness and the gall. I well remember them, and my soul downcast within me. Yet this I call to mind and therefore I have hope: because of the LORD's great love we are not consumed, for his compassions never fail." When you are struggling to focus on God during this season of dead-end life, then take heart: do not lose your hope, because you are not alone. Help is on the way to reverse your circumstances. "[T]hose who hope in the LORD will renew their strength. They will soar on wings like eagles; they will run and not grow weary; they will walk and not be faint (Isa 40:30)."

"I will wait on the LORD, who hides His face from the house of Jacob; and I will hope in Him" (Isa 8:17 NKJV). Hoping for God means fully entrusting our lives to Him. It also includes seeing Him as the source of help and grace when needed. "Hope does not disappoint (Rom 5:5 NKJV)." If you do not hope, then you will be disappointed. In hope, God promises:

1. the power of God to refresh us amid trials, temptations, and suffering
2. the ability to overcome our problems, like an eagle that flies up into the sky and,
3. the ability to run spiritually without feeling tired, and to keep going forward without feeling tired, as God sustains us with His help.

God promises that if we patiently rely on Him, then He will give whatever we need to sustain us.

Waiting upon the Lord takes patience and strong faith in God. Choose to have faith in God when you cannot see through the fog of your circumstances. In waiting, God works for good, even when you do not realize it. Waiting is not a vain work. In waiting, God is willing to reveal His will. However, you also must be willing to submit your will to God. Submitting will cost you everything in your life. Submitting includes a total surrender to life purification. We will not be better people overnight. We must go through a process, which can cause pain. In Joseph's story, there was a reason for Joseph to feel bitterness and hatred against his siblings when they threw him into the pit. However, Joseph refused to allow bitterness to overtake his life. Joseph did not seem to fight back and grumble against his brothers. He may have known that when he would grumble, he would be grumbling against God. He left behind the preferential treatment that he used to receive from his father, and Joseph allowed hardship to shape him. Joseph's attitude led him to see God's marvelous hand working in his life.

Like Joseph, when suffering, Jesus did not fight back and grumble. The Scripture confirms this in 1 Peter 2:23: "When they hurled their insults at him, he did not retaliate; when he suffered, he made no threats. Instead, he entrusted himself to him who judges justly." As the Son of God, Jesus could have defended Himself from suffering and from losing His reputation, but He " . . . Did not consider equality with God something to be used to his own advantage." Jesus, " . . . Humbled himself by becoming obedient to death— even death on a cross! (Phil 2:6-8)." The willingness of Jesus to bear the bitterness of the suffering on the cross makes us have a better life.

One of the most difficult things is to let go of what we have been holding to so dearly, not because we want to, but because we have to. We tend to resist the disruptive moment. This could lead to an angry heart, disappointments, and bitterness in life. In other words, we must allow ourselves to be refined for God's better purpose. The Scripture says, "This third I will put into the fire; I will refine them like silver and test them like gold. They will call on my name and I will answer them; I will say, 'They are my people,' and they will say, 'The LORD is our God (Zech 13:9).'" It does say fire, and this is a dreadful process. However, God's refinery will not destroy us totally, like the fire of an incinerator. Rather, it is the process of removing impurities to bring the silver and gold to their purity. The separation of the impurities from silver and gold makes these metals more valuable. The test of fire is God's ultimate process for shaping us into His image. God is by no means finished with us. Therefore, God may sometimes turn up the heat to accomplish His purpose in us.

You may not like purifying fire, but it is a process of skimming off the impure from the heart to make it into a pure heart. We must be refined like gold. He is God, and the end of all our trials and sufferings will be to the praise, honor, and glory of Jesus. David Jeremiah adds, "The heat of suffering is a refiner's fire, purifying the gold of godly character and wisdom."[2] God is shaping and molding us to become better, and pain is one of the tools that He uses. Gold would never become pure if it never went through the fire. If you want to shine like gold, then you must be willing to go through the furnace.

You see, the test of purification is not without purpose—it is to make us better and to make us shine like gold. Peter endorses that this purification will lead to victory. He puts it like this: "Pure gold put in the fire comes out of it proved pure; genuine faith put through this suffering comes out proved genuine (1 Pet 1:7 MSG)." Going through hardship and suffering, but still mocked by his friends, Job says, "But he knows the way that I take; when he has tested me, I will come forth as gold (Job 23:10)." Job was convinced that God still cared about his life, and Job knew that no misery could make him turn from loyalty to God. "When Jesus wraps this all up, it's your faith, not your gold, that God will have on display as evidence of his victory (1 Pet 1:7 MSG)."

Peter says that suffering, trials, and hardships are tests to prove our faith in order to better us. The purpose of this is to refine our lives, to help us have stronger faith, and to develop the character of God. The test will not disable us but enable us to do better. James says, "Blessed is the one who perseveres under trial because, having stood the test, that person will receive the crown of life that the Lord has promised to those who love him (Jas 1:12)." James encourages us to hang in there during pain and hardship, because we are going to be ordained as champions once we have persevered under pressure. There is power in perseverance. Do not give up. God uses pain as an ornament to beautify your life. There is a saying that, "In the race between lion and deer, many times the deer wins. Because the lion runs for food, while the deer runs for life." Purpose of life is more important than need. The most disabling life is not one in which you cannot walk physically or talk eloquently, but is one in which you do not have a purpose in life. The deer runs for his life. His purpose is not to be killed by the lion. God did not intend your affliction and hardship to devour you. You are called according to God's purpose. Pain has its own purpose. God not only knows better about you, but He is also willing to make you better. He is willing to make you a better person, right after your adversity.

You have heard that all things do work together for good (Rom 8:28). This includes your pain and adversity. Your pain can bring peace, and your adversity can produce prosperity. This Scripture is very comforting for God's children when they have to suffer in this life. God will bring good from all distress, trials, persecutions, and suffering to make us into the image of Christ and, ultimately, to produce our glory. God can reverse your bitterness to make you become better. The prophet Isaiah says it profoundly: "Behold, it was for my peace that I had great bitterness: but thou hast in love to my soul delivered it from the pit of corruption (Isa 38:17 ASV)." Isaiah acknowledged that the pain that he went through eventually gave him a true peace and victorious life. God's love brought his life back from the pit of destruction to the palace of restoration. Isaiah did not hold any grudges but gave himself a chance to be delivered by God's love from the pit of bitterness to the mountain of happiness.

A seemingly unending trial may result in bitterness; however, to become bitter for the rest of your life is a foolish decision. King Solomon, the wise man, reminds us of the effect of making a bad decision, "A person's own folly leads to their ruin, yet their heart rages against the LORD (Prov 19:3)." In the hearts of angry people, they practice ungodliness, and they do not have clean hearts as a tool to regain what has been lost. David realized what had been lost in his life, and he wanted God to restore it. David realized that if he hardened his heart, then his storm could be worse. With an honest heart, David asked God to give him a pure heart and to restore him: "Create in me a pure heart, O God, and renew a steadfast spirit within me. Do not cast me from your presence or take your Holy Spirit from me. Restore to me the joy of your salvation and grant me a willing spirit, to sustain me (Ps 51:10-12)." David wanted to be revived again from his low point in order to enjoy a victory one more time. He realized that a bitter spirit would hinder him in rising. Unresolved resentment and anger, and continued disappointment can cause us to plunge more deeply into a pit.

David experienced being in bitter spirit, and in this experience, he sought a remedy to overcome it. That remedy was none other than God and His word. Jesus Himself did not feel angry and bitter when He went to the cross. Jesus accepted the cross willingly, and He submitted His life to the will of the Father in order that many people would be saved through His suffering on the cross.

Paul encourages us to cast aside bitterness: "Get rid of all bitterness, rage and anger, brawling and slander, along with every form of malice (Eph 4:31)." Bitterness can infiltrate every area of your life. Therefore, you must do away with any bitterness in your heart so that the Lord can bring you to a better life. If someone caused your pain and suffering, then choose to be free from that person and do not hold onto bitterness. You are not condoning the behavior of that person! However, you are allowing yourself to move forward by letting go.

Solomon adds, "Each heart knows its own bitterness, and no one else can share its joy (Prov 14:10)." Bitterness cannot give a joyful life. Choose to become better and to reject bitterness. Be free today from bitterness and be better!

God created you to conquer Satan (who holds you down), so that you can become better.

Welcome Your New Breakthrough and Reject Your Setback

There are two choices when pain strikes: become a victim and stay in grief, or choose to be a victor and feel relief. The time to grieve and regret the dry life is over. Regret can be devastating if you do not keep it in check. The Bible refers to regret as a way for Satan to get inside you mentally. You must move on and finish the race. Do not allow regret to take charge—it only limits your movement. Live with no regrets, but look forward, because your better life is coming, and your fear and pain will be nothing in comparison with your better life. Your progress is better than your regret. Your regret is your past, and God can beautify your past because God is greater than your regret. God never stops chasing you to change you. Do not look at what Satan did, but look to what God is going to do. The moment you start walking, the door will open. Keep walking. Never miss your moment again. Do not stop walking and dreaming, because there is still a good life worth living and pursuing.

After four months in the hospital, I had to undergo a shoulder surgery. At the same time, I had to undergo physiotherapy treatments on my burns even before they were fully dry. Physiotherapy and scar control measures are important for burn victims in order to avoid deformity. I remember the nurse giving me a spoon and a fork. She asked me to practice eating by holding a spoon and a fork, but I could not even hold them. I noticed that my finger skin was bleeding. This was a setback. However, the nurse kept forcing me to do this—if I wanted my hand and finger functions to return to normal. I decided to use my fingers and to fight every day. I refused to let my hands and fingers be crippled.

Your pain and trials are of no value to hold on to. They are your old experiences. Do not look to them. They are instruments used by God to help you reach your new breakthrough. Do not listen to the whisperer who says to go back to your old life. Say to your past, "I am not going back, but I am moving forward." Your past was not your prison for a life sentence. Rather, it is a lesson for an encouragement. In the book of Ruth, we read the story of Naomi who went to a foreign land, together with her husband and their two sons, due to a famine in her land. She and her family were expecting a better life in a foreign land. However, after ten years of living in the foreign land, tragedy struck her family. Naomi's husband and two sons died. Her life was afflicted severely, and she was devastated to the point of rejecting being called her real name: Naomi, which means sweet. She wanting to be called Mara, which means bitter. In bitterness she said, "Don't call me Naomi . . . . Call me Mara because the Almighty has made my life very bitter (Ruth 1:20)." However, amid her brokenness, she refused to give up, and later she declared the goodness of God (Ruth 2:20). Though Naomi felt that God had turned His back on her, she returned to the land of promise to enjoy God's provision one more time. Naomi left her bitterness behind, and she kept moving forward.

When you move forward, things may not line up as you expect. However, when you are willing to move forward, then God will open the way as you never thought before. A. J. Russell writes an encouraging word, saying, "Go forward fearlessly. Do not think about the Red Sea that lies ahead. Be very sure that when you come to it the waters will part and you will pass over to your promised land of freedom."[3]

James R. Sherman's wise words say, "You can't go back and make a new start, but you can start right now and make a brand-new ending"[4] There is no life when you go back to your past. Remember: after meeting Jesus, all His disciples who used to be fishermen agreed to leave their old profession as fishers of fish, and they turned to become fishers of men. However, after Jesus had risen from the dead, Jesus appeared to the disciples for the third time, and He found them fishing, because they did not know what to do (John 21:1-14). Those who were fishing as fishermen, like Simon Peter, Thomas, Nathanael, and two other disciples, went back to their old lifestyle of fishing in the sea of Galilee, but they did not get any fish. They did not recognize and welcome Jesus and make new headway. Jesus had to reassure them again for a total commitment and devotion to love their new calling.

There is no value, no gain, and no profit in the past, especially when God has asked you to leave it behind. There is no room for the old anymore. There is nothing in the past mindset and lifestyle. Life must move forward for the better. Paul understood how the old life must be left behind in order to welcome the new life when he said, "Therefore, if anyone is in Christ, he is a new creation. The old has passed away; behold, the new has come (2 Cor 5:17 ESV)."

Do not allow your pain to hold up your breakthrough. God did not design you to regret your pain, but to greet your progress. God will bring good from all trials, persecutions, and suffering. The difficulties, troubles, hardships, persecutions, famine, nakedness, and danger, listed by Paul in Romans 8:35, have been experienced by God's people throughout the ages. Believers should not be surprised if they experience difficulties, persecution, hunger, poverty, or danger. All of these do not mean that God has left you or that He does not love you anymore. On the contrary, your pain and suffering will open a new breakthrough to experience God's strength and richness to fulfill His great plan in you.

Paul assures that all these difficulties will be overcome, and that we will be more than winners through Christ (Rom 8:37-39). A test is a trial, as well as a temptation, to verify your quality and to establish your reliability. It is never too late to get another new breakthrough. Your pain is an investment for your development.

In the past, you were sick, hurting, and bitter. Today, though, today God is offering you a great breakthrough. Everything is being reversed by the invisible hand of God. This is because God works surpassing all your understanding and anything that you ever imagined (Phil 4:5-7). The voice that tells you that you are a failure should only remind you who you are in God's hands. Do not fear failure but be terrified of regret. God's hand keeps you from sinking under your pain and keeps you from bitterness. Do not get mad at your past, it was only a trigger for better. Do better and rise above. God does not use your past to determine your future. Your pain does not dictate where you are going. What seems as bitter pain often turns out to be a new breakthrough. Be engulfed in your breakthrough and forget that your pain ever happened. Your enrichment and breakthrough are in your heart, not in your circumstances. Your circumstances may overwhelm you, but take the attitude that you will get through it.

You may have lost your health for a while. You may have been left by your friends or even family, and may have been betrayed by someone you love and been hurt. However, do not let your heart be disappointed and bitter because your breakthrough and promotion depends on your big heart. No one can take the hidden things in your heart. To experience a new breakthrough, you must be able to handle your loss. If God wants you to handle more than what you think you can handle, then this means that God will help you handle it. When you have successfully handled your worst, then you have the right to welcome your best. When you lose something in your life, God wants you to pick up something else. He is willing to replace something that you lost for something greater.

Moving Forward With a New Testimony

There was a time when Jesus' disciples caught nothing during the whole night on the Sea of Galilee (John 21:1-3). Having experienced this dry season, it was obvious that their past experiences could not guarantee their future. There is no new life if you are stuck in the old past. God is a good God, but there comes a time when He asks us to change our choices. The disciples of Jesus proved this. They became so dried and empty in hope. No bright future—no enthusiasm, no enjoyment, no provision—only an empty net. Why? Because they tried to stay in their old passion and did not move forward to enjoy a better provision that God had in store for them through their new calling.

However, when Jesus appeared to them in the morning, they heard His words, which were a sign of a new breakthrough. They not only heard this, but they experienced it. But how? The breakthrough only happened when they heard and obeyed the instruction of Jesus: "Throw your net on the right side of the boat and you will find some [fish]."

"When they did, they were unable to haul the net in because of the large number of fish (John 21:6)." Jesus made Himself known again to His disciples, and they were willing to change what they were doing to the new way of what Jesus told them. When they employed Jesus' way in their fishing business, then their efforts produced a boat-sinking catch, a bright future, new enthusiasm, and a new testimony.

Your efforts could lead to visible and desirable changes in your life, as well as in the lives of others. Your pain could change and impact a lot of people for the better. They will bear testimony to save many people from going under. You may still carry the pain, but when you guard your mind and not fill it with pain, then it will not be long until your pain will lead to an amazing testimony. Your mind/thinking determines your attitude, and your attitude will determine your altitude. When your mind embraces a right choice, then you will walk in the right courses. Your pain is not your path—it is only your past. Solomon says, "More than anything you guard, protect your mind, for life flows from it (Prov. 4:23 CEB)." Another translation says it this way: "Be careful what you think, because your thoughts run your life (Prov 4:23 NCV)." Solomon was asking us not to allow our minds to be corrupted by anything. You have many thoughts. However, just because you have negative thoughts does not mean that you have to dwell on them. You can pick what you ponder. You are not the victim of your thoughts. The mind is the source of desires and decisions. Choose to have a sound mind that can alleviate your pain. Do not allow your mind to be robbed by pain that produces a bad report, rather than a good report. Your pain can be an affirmation of your self-formation. Your pain story can turn to a great declaration of a big victory.

The negative thoughts that you think against yourself are the negative seeds that cause damage to yourself. In fact, God gives you many positive views, even when your life is filled with tragedy or difficulties. God tells you good things. Keep in mind that your negative thoughts affect all aspects of your life. To consider yourself not good enough is a view that is contrary to God's view of you. The truth is that God loves you very much.

The paralyzed man who was healed by Jesus is another example of someone who was willing to move forward with his beautiful testimony. When the man was healed, Jesus reminded him not to go back to his old life. Jesus said, "See, you are well again. Stop sinning or something worse may happen to you." The man went away and told the Jewish leaders that it was Jesus who had made him well (John 5:14-15). The man refused to be bound to his past and made himself available for God's testimony to these Jewish leaders.

Allowing your mind to be bombarded by negative thoughts will paralyze you, and this paralysis will limit you from moving forward. Press on toward the goal because a new path of life is awaiting you. Your pain soon will be turned into an awesome testimony. Never think that your testimony is insignificant. Someone out there needs it. Paul put it this way: ". . . But I press on, that I may lay hold of that for which Christ Jesus has also laid hold of me. Brethren, I do not count myself to have apprehended; but one thing *I do*, forgetting those things which are behind and reaching forward to those things which are ahead, I press toward the goal for the prize of the upward call of God in Christ Jesus. Therefore, let us, as many as are mature, have this mind (Phil 3:12-15 NKJV)."

But how do you move forward with a new testimony? Change the old to the new. To do this, you must be willing to burn the bridge behind you. Destroy it so that you cannot return to the old. Cut off the access to the past so that your mind does not live in it anymore. When you live in the past for too long, you open your mind to your emotional turmoil. The devil will keep reminding you of what you are going through and what you have gone through, bringing back bad memories that will tear you apart. The enemy is working to take you back to the old, and is not wanting to see you testify of your victory. The devil attacks those who are next in line for a victory. The devil wants you to remain a loser.

Do not use your pain as an excuse not to reach your shining future. Many people who have been struck by trials have realized their pain was a divine moment. They did not want to waste the pain. Rather, they used it as an opportunity to shine through. Burn the bridges behind you that allow you to keep going back to the same pain, wound, and resentment. Burning your bridge behind you is to rescue you from falling apart further and allow you to move forward to another level. Do not look back. It is impossible to look forward and to look backward at the same time. Let me remind you of Lot's wife's story in Genesis 19:15-26. When the angels of God went to warn Lot and his family to leave the city of Sodom and Gomorrah, because God was about to destroy the city, one of the angels said: "Flee for your lives! Don't look back, and don't stop anywhere in the plain! Flee to the mountains, or you will be swept away (v. 17)." Lot and his daughters ran away and never looked back, but Lot's wife looked back. Lot's wife became a pillar of salt. The obedience of Lot and his daughters saved them, but the disobedience of Lot's wife caused her to lose her life. Your pain is not a reason to disobey God. God allows it for your good, and He expects you to display His character in it.

The airplane accident left me with severe scars on my body and legs. It also left me sometimes feeling nervous when an airplane experiences turbulence in the air. However, I refuse to be haunted by this. I accept my body as what it is, and I keep flying. I realize that my scars are nothing compared to the scars of Jesus that He received while on the cross to save me. Looking back at my horrible experience in the airplane crash only makes me feel frustrated. I refuse to have aviophobia (fear of flying), as many people have. I realize that when I fly, there are storms around in the sky. However, I also realize that God surrounds me with His mighty hands, and I am in good hands. I burned that bridge behind me so I would not be tempted to go back to my past. I wake up every morning and see the scars on my body, but I really am not bothered too much by them anymore. I know that some day my body will be done away with. I saw many burn survivors even worse than me. Living with scars just gives me a chance to say, "Thank you, Lord," because not everyone has this second chance.

As an airplane crash survivor, I take my testimony all over the world to encourage others to keep flying. Christine Caine, an Australian activist, evangelist, author, and international speaker tells her story of her horrific experience when she and her husband flew from Chicago, Illinois, to Raleigh, North Carolina. She says that only twenty minutes after the airplane was airborne, the pilot suddenly announced that the airplane needed to turn around and try to land in Chicago due to having trouble getting the landing gear up.[5] She panicked and was terrified. Since then, she admits that she had terror and anxiety even a week before flying. She felt fear break out every time she thought about getting on a plane. Her heart would begin to race, and her chest would tighten. She admits that fear made her feel fatigued every time she arrived at her destination.[6] However, that terrorized feeling does not stop her from flying. Caine has to go to wherever the doors open to testify to the goodness of God and to preach the Gospel. But it also means she has to fly. Her fear does not stop her from going and helping people hear the good news of grace.[7]

You see, every fear, accident, trial, or pain has a purpose. My pain changed my life, and changed lives are dramatic testimonies to the world. The world desperately needs grace and mercy, and God uses you as a witness to show others how this grace and mercy operate. I am not trying to compare my own experiences with Mrs. Caine's experiences. The good news was that her fear of an airplane crash did not take place, like mine, where many people were injured and died including five Australian high-ranking officers. Mrs. Caine was able to overcome her past fear and to take her testimony to the world. It does not matter how dramatic an accident you went through, or how severe an illness, or how much pain you feel. All that pain is the best testimony to encourage people. When your test turns into a testimony, then it will be a comfort for others' afflictions.

You ask: How can I make a testimony while I am still in pain? I am glad you asked. The best testimony that you can make is when you are in pain. Many people could not make it. They succumb to their situations. It is easier to declare something that you already possess, but not something that is still out of your reach. You cannot give what you do not have. You have pain, and you can share your pain. When you comfort others, you will be comforted.

John Henry Jowett said, "God does not comfort us to make us comfortable, but to make us comforters."[8] People who have not been in pain have little consolation to give. They hardly can inspire the sufferer. Therefore, when you are not in pain yet, or have not gone through pain, then you do not have any empathy with those who are in pain. Empathy is borne out of experience. Experience in the furnace of affliction, and witnessing of God's faithfulness and timely deliverance, are all designed to equip us, to comfort us, and to give us hope. "After all, it is difficult for us to help those who are in trouble if we have not been there before."[9] Paul says, "Praise be to the God and Father of our Lord Jesus Christ, the Father of compassion and the God of all comfort, who comforts us in all our troubles, so that we can comfort those in any trouble with the comfort we ourselves receive from God (2 Cor 1:3-4)."

Referring to what Paul says in this passage, T. D. Jakes, a pastor and author, tells his encouraging testimony: "Throughout [the book] *Crushing* and throughout my ministry, I have tried to be authentic. I often use examples of my own life trials to illustrate sermons and stories in my books. I believe if anything is worth sharing from the pulpit, . . . then it must be authentic to my own experience. . . . people wonder how I, a man of God, could be so deflated, discouraged, doubtful, and even depressed when certain events hit me and crushed me. How can I feel trapped in my pain . . . ? [Like others,] I'm equally susceptible to suffering. However, [during my trials] I have learned what Paul wrote about . . . . [T]the comforting words or comforting lessons . . . are exactly what can help others as they go through their trials. In essence, I am comforted so I can comfort others. My trials are not just for me. The things I learn through my trials can help strengthen someone else in the midst of their trials." Jakes points out that we come through those things to be able to relate to others.[10]

Do not isolate yourself; rather, reach out to people and let your pain encourage others. The Scripture says, "The human spirit can endure in sickness, but a crushed spirit who can bear? (Prov 18:14)" As you draw your strength from God, your spirit will be able to bear you up in your pain. The wellspring of strength will flow from your heart. Your strength is a testimony that could uplift others from their discouragement. The best testimony that you can give is to encourage others while you need encouragement. You will be surprised to see that you will receive encouragement while you encourage others. One day, a pastor came to my hospital and prayed for me. After he finished praying, the Lord moved my heart to pray for the pastor as well. The pastor told my wife that he felt so blessed and encouraged, and that he never had the experience where the sick person prayed for the healthy person. You see, while in pain, you can still be an encourager to others. Pain is not a drawback to being used by God but is an opportunity. Pain is not a drawback, but an opportunity that can be used by God to strengthen and benefit others.

Talk with others who have gone through similar experiences. When you meet with others who share the same pain, it helps to heal your wounds and others' wounds. Sympathy is born of experience. Jesus Himself sympathizes with our weaknesses (Heb 4:15). Even when we experience distress, He too is distressed (Isa 63:9). Paul learned from the many hardships that he experienced, and he was driven to share this with others who were in hardship. In 2 Corinthians 1:3-7, Paul says:

> Praise be to the God and Father of our Lord Jesus Christ, the Father of compassion and the God of all comfort, who comforts us in all our troubles, so that we can comfort those in any trouble with the comfort we ourselves receive from God. For just as we share abundantly in the sufferings of Christ, so also our comfort abounds through Christ. If we are distressed, it is for your comfort and salvation; if we are comforted, it is for your comfort, which produces in you patient endurance of the same sufferings we suffer. And our hope for you is firm, because we know that just as you share in our sufferings, so also you share in our comfort.

Paul demonstrates how God uses his sufferings and trials to strengthen others. You are called to uplift one another. Your pain is a powerful testimony of God's power. Your wound can be a healing power to heal others' wounds. Your pain creates a compassionate heart in you and gives you a depth of understanding about other people's pain. The compassionate heart shaped by pain drives you to testify about your pain in order to motivate others.

Chapter 9

LIFE BEYOND SURVIVAL

*"··· I press on to make it my own, because Christ
Jesus has made me his own. ... .. But one thing I do:
forgetting what lies behind and straining forward to
what lies ahead, I press on toward the goal for the
prize of the upward call of God in Christ Jesus."*
(Philippians 3:12-14 ESV)

For to me, to live is Christ and to die is gain"
(Philippians 1:21)

I survived the horrible airplane crash that almost took my
life. I celebrate my life and the lives of others who have
been given an opportunity for a second chance to live on
this earth. I give thanks to my protector, God Almighty. I
am proud to say, "I am a survivor by the grace of God." To
those who have been given a second chance to survive, I am
encouraging you: Do not waste your second chance. To those
who have not gone through a near-death experience, I am

encouraging you never to waste your first chance, because your second chance might never come. Many people do not get a second chance to survive. Although they were trying to hold on for years, they still do not make it. They cannot survive it. If you are a cancer survivor, accident survivor, or other hardship survivor, then be thankful and celebrate it.

However, being in a survival mode is not enough—you must arise. To arise is an overcomer's attitude. Getting a second chance to live is one thing; making it a better life is another thing. Being an overcomer is the way to make a better life. A survivor is only able to self-defend against the attacker, but the overcomer will arise and defeat the attacker. A survivor tells of how s/he went through a fire, suffered from it, and became a victim of it; however, an overcomer tells of how s/he escaped from fire, arose from it and the suffering, and became a victor. The overcomers give themselves a chance to be fed by the mighty power of God in order to rise and to have the attitude of winning.

Being a survivor is an opportunity to receive, but being an overcomer is the ability to receive and to give. The Scripture says, "He who has an ear, let him hear what the Spirit says to the churches. To him who overcomes I will give to eat from the tree of life, which is in the midst of the Paradise of God (Rev 2:7 NKJV)." The overcomer will be rewarded with a tree of life and be enabled to share life. The overcomer desires to leave a legacy to other survivors, as well as to be engaged with others' pain. God is shouting to you in this season in order to wake you up and to move you to another level of your victory. When you break, it does not mean that you are not useful anymore. You should try to resuscitate yourself. This is the essence of resilience.

Being a survivor is a precious gift, but being an over-comer is an even more beautiful gift, presented as fruit to God and shared with other people. The reason behind your survival is because God knows that you have the ability to reach His given purpose and potential to their fullness. Therefore, leave survival mode, and move forward to live beyond it.

In his book *Living Beyond Survival*, Van Johns speaks from his experience as a victim of family abusive treatment and says, "We know that victims learn to survive for years while suppressing their hidden tragedies. We who have been victims must learn to live beyond survival by turning tragedy into hope. We must learn to outlive our oppressors without fear."[1] Johns tells those who have been repeatedly mentally or physically abused not to give up on life but to seek comfort. "Learning to acknowledge the spiritual presence of God, listening to the teachings, reading and studying the Bible, self-help books, in addition to interacting with positive people doing positive things, has been paramount in reinforcing my faith—to live life beyond survival."[2]

Your survival could turn out better than you imagine. Jeremiah says, "Thus says the LORD, 'The people who survived the sword found grace in the wilderness—Israel, when it went to find its rest (Jer 31:2 NASU).'" Israel would return to the Promised Land after they survived in the wilderness. Israel would once again live together under God's blessing. After convincing them of this recovery, Jeremiah stated that God would make a better new covenant with His people, which would include spiritual power to obey His commandments. Beyond the hardships in the wilderness, God promised something better for them.

To survive is to know what God has in store for you in the next life journey. Life must move on, ready to face another hit, maybe an even harder hit. To be able to take another hit, you must go beyond the survival mode of the present pain. Keep in your heart that you have the potential to conquer every hardship and trial.

When David was in big trouble because of the mistakes he made, he not only asked God to give him strength to handle his situation, but David asked God for total restoration and a steadfast spirit to support him for his next step (Ps 51:10). David did not just want to regain his salvation and hang in there. Rather, David desired a new heart to move on. David not only asked God to fix his problem, but to change his heart to see the way that God sees, and to do things the way that God does. David was willing to see things from the right perspective of God. David wanted to revive again from his low point in order to enjoy his next victory. To do this, David wanted to go beyond his current situation.

Do not be stuck in your current situation and be content there. Make up your mind and do something. The best is still to come. Give yourself a chance to embrace it. God loves you just the way you are, and He can fix you just the way you are. God not only wants you to exist, but to be excellent. However, to be excellent is not to look for a quick fix. The lame man had been waiting a long time to arise, but after thirty-eight years, his arising finally came about (John

5:1-9). He was stepping forward, embracing his new life, leaving his old crippled mindset behind, and proclaiming the power of his Healer. The lame man desired to live beyond being a crippled survivor, and he was ready to live to as a herald of Jesus' healing. This man not only received healing, but he became a voice of the Healer. "The man went away and told the Jewish leaders that it was Jesus who had made him well (John 5:15)."

The Scripture gives us an encouraging word to move on exceedingly: "Forget the former things; do not dwell on the past. See, I am doing a new thing! Now it springs up; do you not perceive it? I am making a way in the wilderness and streams in the wasteland (Isa 43:18-19)." Even in a dry land there will be a spring of water that gives life. There will be a way for the impossible. Hope is birthed from hopelessness. Never lose hope! It is time to stand up strong and to welcome your excellent new life and new hope. You are not a prisoner of your pain and your pain is not a life sentence. It was just a good lesson to learn from.

Paul understood that suffering, trials, and diseases cause pain, but that pain can bring about change. After going through suffering and hardship, many people become men and women of character who were shaped by pain. Paul invites us to believe that there is a new hope and a new life following suffering: "Not only so, but we also glory in our sufferings, because we know that suffering produces perseverance; perseverance, character; and character, hope. And hope does not put us to shame, because God's love has been poured out into our hearts through the Holy Spirit, who has been given to us (Rom 5:3-5)."

There is a reason for you to be a survivor. God did this for a reason. Pain and suffering do not put you into a shameful situation. You must be proud of it, because God knows that you are the one who can handle it, and He uses it to change you for the better. It is a time for change and time to move on. Do not live as though nothing happened to you. You have gone through it. God has granted you a bulldog type of faith, and this is why you made it. Hence, your survival is not for the average life, but for an excellent life. Allow your pain to trigger your empathy and allow it to impact someone's life. You are the recipient of God's grace.

A beautiful story of a survivor came from Jason Koger. Jason is a trauma survivor and upper extremity amputee. While riding an ATV around his grandfather's farm, Jason came in contact with a power line that was down. 7200 volts of electricity rushed through his body, leading to severe traumatic injuries. Jason was air lifted to the burn unit to get medical treatment. In order to save his life, both of Jason's hands were amputated, and he was placed in an induced coma for 3 days. When starting the recovery process, Jason decided to not give up. He shares that every day, he woke up and thought of goals that he wanted to reach. Those goals started out as feeding himself and dressing himself. While going through therapy and working through challenges, Jason started to move forward. Now Jason enjoys helping amputees and other survivors be successful. He is a motivational speaker and loves giving back. Jason is proud to be a survivor and to encourage other survivors that even after trauma, life can still be good.[3] Jason has dedicated his life to empowering others and becoming a healing vessel.

Like Jason, you do not want to see yourself and other survivors being stuck in survival celebration activities and in being content in a survival mode. Feeling contented is not the only reason to be a survivor. The impact on others of your surviving is the best reason to be a survivor. Therefore, surviving must be followed by the making of a sacrifice to determine your success. You have a right to celebrate your survival, but do not stay in that comfort zone. Satisfaction is what makes you stuck, but sacrifice is what makes you have success. Do not sacrifice your time, energy, and mind by going back to the past and being haunted by pain. There is a purpose for your survival. The purpose of your life transcends your hardships and suffering. Pain is not always a bad thing. Rather, it is a trigger to take action for the best thing in life. Life is an opportunity. God has an eternal plan that includes all the intentions and activities of everyone on earth. We must offer ourselves to God to be used by Him to carry out His eternal plan for us and through us in order to impact the hurting and to help the helpless. Your courage to take your healing to the world is beyond your survival mode.

Your Decision Determines Your Destiny

Many of the outcomes of our decisions are impossible to predict. We do not fully understand whether our pain was due to our own actions or due to factors beyond our control. As a result, we become nervous about making decisions to answer the many questions that we have had regarding pain. Some questions may have been answered, but other questions remain as puzzles. Do not let your pain remain as a puzzle, and do not deny it. What you can do is remain strong, stay true, and be yourself. Make up your mind concerning your life journey and then determine your actions. Your actions will determine your destiny. Life is decision-making. Do not succumb to your situation, because your situation does not determine who you are. Being stuck in your current situation will not help.

You may not know why you went through trials and hardship, but you must make a decision to move forward. You cannot buy time, but you still have time. The decision to move forward must be made while we are still living in the present in this life. Your pain is not shutting you down but waking you up. You may be hurt, but not broken. However, even if you are broken, God does not neglect brokenness. You may fall many times. However, get up and rise to another level, because God is still on His throne watching over you. The most disabling life is not because you cannot walk physically, but because you cannot walk to your destiny. Make a decision and take an action. Paul encourages us to fight the good fight of faith and to take hold of the eternal life to which you were called (1 Tim 6:12). The Scripture encourages us to withstand to the end when it says that, "The one who endures to the end will be saved (Matt 24:13 ESV)."

There is a choice that you have to make: either believe that only a broken life is ahead of you or believe that a bright future is waiting for you. Making a choice to live beyond survival is the right decision, because your pain is part of the journey that leads to your destiny. Your pain is not your destination. Your current situation is used to fight for your destination. You may not realize it now, but God uses it to pave the way to your destiny. Your situation may get worse before it gets better, but Jesus is on both ends of it. Jesus empathizes with our weaknesses/infirmities (Heb 4:15), and He will not allow your infirmity to stop your destiny. Walk a little farther, and do not depend on your bad feeling. Walking with your bad feelings only makes you a victim of falling. Do not rely on your feelings, because this only causes nervousness. Rather, rely on God, and He will give you confidence. Rise up one more time, and do not allow your pain to intimidate you. Your pain and adversity are not your failures. They prepare you for a remarkable destiny. You may think that you have failed this time. However, if you do your best, then God's eyes are watching every bit of your journey. The Israelites were not destined just to be survivors in the wilderness. They were destined to be a victorious nation. The wilderness may be a part of the journey, but the promised land is the destiny. Therefore, the cruel Pharaoh's army could not hold them, the deadly Red Sea could not swallow them, the torrential Jordan river could not drown them, and all the enemies that surrounded Israel could not destroy them. The reason is because they were not destined to end in the land of wilderness, but in the land of promise. Pharaoh's cruel army behind, the massive Red Sea in front, and the torrential Jordan River ahead of the Hebrews were big problems for them. However, for God, these were not big deals, because God knew it, and He is in control. These situations were all permitted and designed by God as means for the Israelites to reach their destiny. God was working behind the scene without being seen by Israel's natural eyes.

There is blessing in disguise behind your pain. There is a greater purpose beyond pain. God has prepared you, and He is leading you to reach your destiny, and you need to make a choice with the right decision. The Scripture says, "I have set before you life and death, blessing and cursing; therefore choose life, that both you and your descendants may live; that you may love the LORD your God, that you may obey His voice, and that you may cling to Him, for He *is* your life and the length of your days (Deut 30:19b-20a NKJV)." You see, life is decision-making. God was asking Israel to choose and was encouraging them to choose life rather than death. God wanted Israel to be better and to be blessed, leaving behind bitterness and curses. You must make an effort to discover how to heal while traveling the path from desperation to restoration. To be bitter is desperation, but to be better is restoration.

If you have ever succumbed to your pain in the past, then God wants to see you restored and to rise again even higher. God wants you to leave that disastrous decision and to determine to act in God's direction. God reminded Israel that He would restore their misfortunes into fortunes, and their poverty into prosperity. God had compassion on the

Israelites, and He gathered them again from all the nations where He scattered them. To turn it around, though, Israel had to choose life. There was no life in their past. Do not run back into your familiar world, or old lifestyles, and be defeated. For Israel, living in Egypt was an old life. Walking in the rough desert was a test. God did not want Israel stuck in the same valley of decision between two places. Their decisions determined their destiny, and their destiny was born when they obeyed God's voice and did it His way.

As He did for Israel, God gives you the freedom to make choices about what you think is going to be good, better, or even best for you. However, do not make choices out of anger, regret, rebellion, or as an escape. Rather, make decisions out of obedience to God. Destiny is not born out of anger or disappointment. Obedience determines the benefits that you receive. Leave your self-pity and break forth into your destiny. Expose yourself to the Word of God and allow your mind to be renewed with the Word of God and His wisdom (Rom 12:1-3).

God is willing to turn your adversity into victory, and you must be ready. God is urging you right now to welcome your destiny in Christ. God is opening a new chapter for you. You are not going through the same pain anymore. All you need to do is to push through. Do not quit too soon, otherwise you will lose your momentum. Your momentum is being birthed precisely during this survival time. Like a woman ready to birth her child, you need to push harder and to be ready to give birth to your destiny. Nobody will abort your destiny, and nothing will cancel it—God has already designed and prepared it for you. You just have not seen it yet. Whatever you consider as pain, God will make it as gain. Do not look at your pain, it will only make you stressed. Rather, look to Jesus, because He will make you blessed. Press on, push through, and do not give up. God is watching you and leading you, as you are heading off to your destiny. When you decide to move forward, remember: do not be careless! Satanic warfare will come against you to cancel your destiny, but do not break rank and backslide. The enemy cannot keep you from determining your wonderful path to lead you to your destination.

When Paul demanded to go to Rome to be tried by the Emperor (Acts 25:9-12), in his journey to Rome he went through many hardships and trials. Even before facing trial, he already went through storms, shipwreck, snake bite, and much more. Going through all these hardships, Paul could have given up. But he knew that his last destination was Rome. Paul understood that the level of his adversity was directly proportional to his destiny. He realized that his journey was a part of his destiny and, therefore, Paul was determined to finish it and to remain faithful. You have a purpose and a destiny in Christ Jesus. God destined you to a victorious life, and no pain and trials should keep you from achieving it.

In the midst of my adversity, after I regained conscious-ness from my airplane crash, three days later, the Lord spoke to my heart to leave my job. After a long argument with God, I finally said yes to Him. I left my job as a tax officer, and I went to the mission field to preach the Gospel. I did not realize that I was preparing for my wonderful destiny through my pain. I had to choose. I knew that my destiny was my choice, and God helped me make up my mind concerning my calling that determined the course of my actions, and those actions were to impact my destiny. I made my decision to not regret what had happened to me. I have burned the old bridges behind me, and I have given access to God to intervene in me. God gives me the power to choose, and I have made my decision to cross over my new bridge and to walk on my new path.

Today, I challenge you to make your decision to choose. Do not limit God. He can, and is willing, to do for you. It all depends on what kind of destination you want to reach. As a burn survivor, my challenge to you today is to stop traveling in a direction that brings you back to your sickness, depression, sadness, and pain. These are not your destiny. You are not destined to be a victim of pain. You are destined to be a victor of gain. Your pain is a means used by Satan to discourage you from reaching your destiny. However, God uses it as a tool for preparation. When God opens the way, He will let you stay. God knows that there is potential inside you, and He wants to maximize your potential to its fullness. Pain is just an instrument to redirect your destiny. Choose life that is full of victory, and God has given you a power to control your life. Your painful condition is not your life's conclusion. God can fix the pain and turn it into your beautiful destiny, because you have chosen it by having faith in God, and He is not taking His hand off you.

Live a Radical Life

David Platt says, "Real success is found in radical sacrifice. Ultimate satisfaction is found not in making much of ourselves but in making much of God."[4] Platt goes on to say that there is nothing inherently wrong with the American dream, but let it not overtake our desire for Christ and our fear of living with radical abandonment to Christ for His glory in all the world.[5] The measure of success life is not found in what you have—your health, wealth, or other material things— but in who has you. Christ has you—this is why He loves you and gave you another chance to live. Your health and wealth may someday disappear again, but He who has you will be with you through eternity.

We all desire healing of pain and restoration of hearts. In other words, you want to be healthy, and God will give good health because He wants you to enjoy His unmerited favor. However, your healthy body will only be useable in this world. When your time is up in this world, then you do not need to ask or to pray to God for your body to heal anymore. Pain will not bother you anymore. There will be a time to leave this corrupted body in this world, and to be transformed into a new body that will never suffer from pain. The Scripture confirms this to us, "And God will wipe away every tear from their eyes; there shall be no more death, nor sorrow, nor crying. There shall be no more pain, for the former things are passed away (Rev 21:4 NKJV)." All these painful laboring lives shall pass away for a better life. Paul even assures us that what we suffer now is nothing compared to the glory that God will reveal to us (Rom 8:18).

The passing away of these former things is often accompanied with Solomon's cry of, "Vanity of vanities; all *is* vanity (Eccl 1:2 NKJV)." Solomon reminded us, "There is time for everything, . . . a time to be born and a time to die, . . . a time to kill and a time to heal (Eccl 3:1-3)." We can never go against God's time. The only thing that we can do is to adjust to it. When we are willing to accept God's time, then we can learn to live in it. God is the owner of time. When our time is up, then all our health and wealth will be meaningless. In that day, only our personal relationship with Jesus Christ matters.

Celebrate your life and your healing, but make sure your celebration is followed by dedication. Dedication is the indication of willingness to be transformed to the will of God. You must be willing to move beyond your plan to be healthy physically. There must be a reason why God allows pain and brokenness. No matter how severe the wound, you are still alive as you are reading this book. The pain you bear is not a wasted thing. If you felt weakened as a person by your pain, this is not true. This is a lie from Satan. You may feel discouraged for a while, but the good news is that you are becoming stronger, and it will help you get back on the path of a righteous life to be zealous for God. Seek and you will find Him. Seeking shows an earnest desire accompanied by obedience to God's will. It is difficult to find joy in pain, but you can find joy when you seek it in Christ, the Healer of your body and soul.

You may have a physical drawback, like mine, or even experience a disability that hinders you from living a normal life, as people define it. But what does a normal life mean? Normal life is relative. It depends on how you perceive it. A normal life is not only determined by physical healthiness. Every person has a different kind of disability or handicap in life. The body is a physical form with mechanical processes that can go wrong sometimes. The physical form of a body is determined by many factors from outside. However, how we live is determined by what is within us. Therefore, our physical form should not determine how we live. Normal life is not only determined by physical form, but by the spiritual form that is within us. The spiritual life that is within us creates a normal life. Paul speaks of "Christ in you, the hope of glory (Col 1:27)." Christ came to live in our spirits. He is making His home inside us. The Christ who lives in us is our hope. His presence in our hearts is a healing power for soul/spirit that brings a normal life. When our spirits are healed, then our bodies can also be healed.

The ultimate healing is not only the healing of body, but the healing of the soul/spirit. Paul prays, "May God himself, the God of peace, sanctify you through and through. May your whole spirit, soul and body be kept blameless at the coming of our Lord Jesus Christ (1 Thess 5:23)." You are a spirit being and, therefore, you have the ability to love God and to hear God speak, because God is Spirit. You have a soul (mind, will, and emotions) and, therefore, you have the ability to choose. You live in your body and, therefore, you must present your body as a living sacrifice to God. Paul puts it this way in Romans 12:1-2:

> Therefore, I urge you, brothers and sisters, in view of God's mercy, to offer your bodies as a living sacrifice, holy and pleasing to God— this is your true and proper worship. Do not conform to the pattern of this world but be transformed by the renewing of your mind. Then you will be able to test and approve what God's will is—his good, pleasing and perfect will.

You do not present your body just to be healed physically, but also to be healed emotionally and spiritually, in order to be used for God's glory. You are a spirit being, but you live in your body. Your body is supposed to be a living sacrifice. Paul says, "You were bought with a price. So glorify God in your body (1 Cor 6:20 ESV)." The reason we live in this body is for the purpose of doing the will of God on this earth. You should have a sincere desire to please God in love, devotion, praise, and holiness, and you should offer your body for His service. Your greatest desire should be a holy life that is pleasing to God. This requires separating from the world and getting closer to God. You must live for God and obey Him, and along with God, you must: oppose sin and defend the truth, reject and hate evil, do good works for others, imitate Christ, serve Him, and live according to the Spirit.

Do not make your pain and suffering an excuse to fall into sin against the will of God. Your pain will not keep you from pleasing God, but sin will. Your body may be hurt, but your soul must be continually related to God as the source of your strength. The healing of your soul is so important to God. God is the healer of your body, soul, and spirit. Therefore, God does not want you to be stuck in only being healed physically. You are an eternal being, and you need an eternal perspective. Do not be satisfied to stay on the page of a physical survival level. Do not only seek physical healing and neglect the healing of your soul. Living beyond a survival level means having a desire to be revived in soul, as well as to be new person in spirit. You may not be able to control your circumstances, but you can control your heart. Jesus says, "Let not your heart be troubled, . . . believe also in Me (John 14:1 NKJV)."

Do not choose to live unrighteously because of your unpleasant circumstances. You must be willing to live according to the fundamental truths of God at the expense of the world's beliefs and behaviors. The world has its own pattern, which is to reject suffering and to embrace the sweetness of the world—even if it leads to sin. Change your mind and turn the world upside down, like the followers of Jesus did in Thessalonica (Acts 17). As your mind changes, you will see your life pattern become more radical for Jesus, and you will be able to move beyond your current circumstances.

To move to that level, we must hold onto and relate to the Healer and the Creator. Do not live average—it is too dangerous. The storm is still raging out there. Go higher and move to another level of spiritual life to explore the meaning of life with God. This spiritual life is the energy that enables you to praise God in your storm.

In Matthew 14:13-36, we read that Jesus fed five thousand people, walked on water, and healed the sick. Jesus' disciples just witnessed Jesus doing miracles, as well as feeding five thousand with five loaves and two fish. However, in order to see another miracle performed by Jesus, Peter and the other disciples had to go to the other side of the sea with Jesus, where Jesus healed sick people in all the surrounding countryside. Crossing the sea, though, was not an easy thing. The disciples' boat was tossed about by a storm. Amazingly, Jesus was in the storm to intervene, and after Peter asked to come to Jesus, He called Peter, 'Come!' Peter had to get out of the boat and walk on the water in order to go to Jesus. Peter went to Jesus obediently, and Jesus took hold of Peter when he began to sink. Only when Jesus got into the boat with Peter did the storm stop. Peter and his friends had to experience the storm in order to experience a great miracle. Before they crossed the sea, they only saw physical needs being met, including five loaves and two fish to feed five thousand. On the other side of the sea, though, they saw spiritual needs being fulfilled, when all the people who touched the fringe of Jesus' cloak were made perfectly whole. Jesus' disciples had to experience an extraordinary situation in order to see and to experience an extraordinary spiritual breakthrough done by Jesus on the other side of the sea.

Ordinary people are only ready to face ordinary situations, but extraordinary people are ready for extraordinary lives. Extraordinary life is knowing that you were created as a masterpiece of God. Therefore, love what God loves, do what God does, see what God sees, and feel what God feels. You are a masterpiece in the making. Living an extraordinary life is to know what God wants you to be—and only God can give the extraordinary life that you desire.

An extraordinary life does not come from material success or your prime healthy body. Rather, extraordinary life comes from a radical obedience to God's will. Paul realized that there is a limit to the physical body, but there is a renewal for the spirits of people as he says: "Even though our outward man is perishing, yet the inward *man* is being renewed day by day (2 Cor 4:16 NKJV)." Inward man refers to the human spirit that has the spiritual life of Christ.

When the Spirit of God has renewed your heart, then you know how to do the will of God, because the will of God is in you and for you. You are presenting your body as a pleasing sacrifice to Him, regardless of the condition of your body. If the will of God is done in you and through you, then life will be more meaningful and fulfilling. A radical life needs a total surrender. A total surrender brings a complete life. An unyielding heart will remain broken. A complete life gives the ability to see that life transcends the pain and hardships differently from the way the world sees them, and the ability to discover the true meaning and purpose of life. Only through total surrender will you be able to see life from God's perspective and purpose, as well as to care what God cares about.

David Platt points out what radical life means: "We will discover that our meaning is found in community and our life is found in giving ourselves for the sake of others in the church, among the lost, and among the poor. We will evaluate where true security and safety are found in this world, and in the end we will determine not to waste our lives on anything but uncompromising, unconditional abandonment to a gracious, loving Savior who invites us to take radical risk and promises us radical reward."[6]

When you live a radical life, you want to pursue the heart of Jesus to go out to take His healing to this hurting world. An extraordinary life is a useful life that is rewarded by God, and not by the world. God challenges you to live a super-ordinary life in Him. You do not want to waste the rest of your time in this temporary world. Life is too precious to waste. It would be a grave mistake to live only for yourself.

Life is meant to make an impact—to be useful for God and others. Your life is not only meant to be a seeker of healing, but to be a giver of healing. God does not comfort you just to make you feel comfortable, but rather, to make you be a comforter of others. God needs a good Samaritan today. Leave the life of quiet desperation, and give yourself an opportunity to be bold in Jesus and to proclaim the goodness of God to the broken world.

Many artists, performers, and famous singers pursue Hollywood-style dreams. However, Kanye West, the best-selling musical artist of all time, declared that he no longer cares for fame and money, but is in the service of God. He left his old life and declared to work for God's mission. There is always a turning point in life to pursue a more meaningful life for God and others. When I quit my worldly career, I knew that I would be facing many challenges. However, I was privileged to receive my calling to be able to go out into God's field to discover the meaning of my life among the lost, the hurting, and the poor. A second chance at life was not wasted by me anymore. Rather, it is a chance to use my life to the fullness of God's calling. Though a painful way to live, your pain will never make you the same person anymore. Pain will change your perception about God.

This happened to Dietrich Bonhoeffer, a German Protestant theologian. He was willing to share the trials of German believers in the hands of Nazis. His view of God's grace in a secular world led to his imprisonment and execution at the hands of the Nazi regime. Bonhoeffer saw that the world had misused the meaning of God's grace. "The world goes on in the same old way, in every sphere of life, and does not presumptuously aspire to live a different life under grace."[7] He said that Christians should beware of rebelling against the free and boundless grace of God and desecrating it.[8] For Bonhoeffer, grace is *costly* because it calls us to follow Jesus Christ radically, and we should be willing to pay this costly price because it cost God, the life of His Son.[9]

A Calling from the Highest to the Lowest

Zacchaeus, the tax collector, made a living by collecting more taxes than he should get from the people, and he become rich from his ill-gotten gains (Luke 19:1-10). Because of this, he was looked down on, and he was rejected by the community. Have you been despised and rejected because of what has befallen you? Whether by mistake or intentionally, being despised or rejected is a painful condition.

When I was hospitalized, my nurse told me that the wife of a man—a burn-survivor patient who was next to my room—was despised and rejected by his wife because of his ugly face full of scars. Not patient to wait for such a long process of healing of her husband, eventually the wife ran away and married another man, leaving her helpless husband at a hospital. His physical suffering turned to heartbrokenness. Many people are being bullied, mocked, or despised by friends, or even their own family members, because of physical disfiguring. One of the burn survivors I knew was very frustrated and angry with himself because every time he walked down the street, children ran away from him screaming and scared. His face was full of scars, his ears were missing, and only half of his nose was left.

After three months in the third hospital, my doctor suggested that it was better to stay outside the hospital because the hospital was not really a sterile place for a burn patient like me. My wife took me to a hotel, but I had to see the doctor in the hospital every other day. My wounds were still raw, especially on my bottom and legs, and I could not sit at all. Therefore, the hospital ambulance had to pick me up from the hotel and take me back. Every time I passed the hotel lobby, my wife had to help me walk to the waiting ambulance. People stared at me, wondering what had happened to me. Some of the hotel guests dared to ask my wife what was happening to me. I felt embarrassed and broken, but I had to move on to see my doctor in the hospital.

I know what it means to be at a very low point—it feels hopeless, and you can feel defenseless. Your friends may leave you. Your family may leave your side. Nevertheless, God will never leave your side. He surrounds you with His angels when nobody else is around. God accepts you when many people reject you. Luke 19:1-9 tells of Zacchaeus, who was despised and rejected because of being a tax collector and what he had done. However, despite being despised and rejected by the community, and being labelled as a sinner by the Pharisees, nothing could stop Zacchaeus from his wanting to see Jesus, even to the point of climbing on a tree limb. Zacchaeus knew there was something in the person of Jesus. Zacchaeus needed to see Jesus, regardless of what the community said about him. He did not care what people said about him—he only cared what Jesus had to say about him. Zacchaeus knew that Jesus was the Messiah, the Savior of his soul. Therefore, Zacchaeus did everything to meet Jesus in order to fill the missing part of his soul.

When Jesus came by, He looked up into the tree, and He said, "Zacchaeus, make haste and come down, for today I must stay at your house (Luke 19:5 NKJV)." God chooses things that are despised by the world—things counted as nothing at all—and He uses them to bring to nothing what the world considers important (1 Cor 1:28). God often uses seemingly insignificant things to accomplish His purposes. Do not use your pain, trials, or hardships as reasons to feel like you are despised or rejected. Your pain cannot define you. You have the right to define what you are going to do with your pain. Zacchaeus refused to be despised and rejected by his community, and he went and met with Jesus in his own home.

Zacchaeus desperately needed the Savior of his soul. Zacchaeus had to leave his comfortable office, that caused him to be despised and rejected by the community in order to find the real Comforter of his life and his family. He desired to be accepted by Jesus. Zacchaeus got what he wanted when he emptied and humbled himself, and when he heard a call from the highest place that said, "Zacchaeus . . . today I must stay at your house." Zacchaeus was called from his low point in life to experience his turning point. He realized that when he was down, God could lift him up. Jesus, who was at the highest place, was willing to meet with Zacchaeus. The invitation came to the humbled Zacchaeus. He appreciated the infilling presence of Jesus because he was empty in his heart. Zacchaeus was willing to look up to Jesus because he was down in his heart. Zacchaeus was despised and rejected by the people around him, but Jesus was around to welcome him. Zacchaeus was spiritually poor, but he was enriched by the presence of Jesus. Zacchaeus was hungry, but he was fed by Jesus. Zacchaeus could not wait to have dinner together with Jesus.

Zacchaeus humiliated himself in public by climbing a tree in order to see Jesus. As a chief tax collector, Zacchaeus probably could have invited Jesus to his office. To our amazement, Zacchaeus did not do this. Rather, he left it all behind—

his position, richness, and public position—in order to pursue something more precious to him: a call from the Highest. What Zacchaeus used to be proud of, he now realized as a stigma in the eyes of God. Zacchaeus' heart was broken, and this caused him pain. Zacchaeus may have had a heavy heart because of the accusations against him, but he responded to the call of Jesus with an excellent spirit. Something changed in Zacchaeus' life. He ignored the community's judgement and condemnation, and he turned to Jesus' compliment and endorsement. Therefore, Zacchaeus' hopelessness turned to hope. His heart had been healed, and he could not wait to share it with his family and others. Zacchaeus had a passion to give what he had, instead of getting something from others. When you are still in your brokenness, God calls you in order to use you for His greater purposes. God uses your pain to improve someone else's life.

Three months after the airplane accident, I was in the second hospital, but my burns were still raw and painful. To make it worse, the doctor explained to my wife that the hospital had run out of anti-bacterial medication. Not knowing what to do, but lying in pain in the sterile room, suddenly a man wanted to speak to me from the other side of my room. Using the telephone, I could see him through the glass wall. He explained what had happened to him. I saw some scars in his face, and suddenly he showed me that some of his fingers were missing. Oh my God—someone's scars were worse than mine! He said, "I was one of the Marriott Hotel's bombing victims in Indonesia." He suggested that I needed to go to another hospital for better treatment—the hospital where he was treated. Soon I was moved to the third hospital, which was the hospital that he recommended.

God sent someone to encourage me. God used that person's pain to help heal my pain. The bombing survivor did not hide himself, but he went out to support others, and God sent him to me that day. You never know who will be sent by God to you in your pain today, and whose pain will be healed through you today. God uses your pain in His way to elevate you and others to a higher level. Be ready to share your pain with whoever asks, and be ready to listen to someone else's pain. Many people long to be heard and need to be encouraged. You can be that person who is used by God through your pain and brokenness.

Zacchaeus was not in physical pain, but he was broken in heart. He had a lot of money to spend to care for his physical health. However, feeling hated, condemned, despised, and empty caused him to be broken. Most of us do not want to be broken. The world despises the broken. Even family members, like the wife of the burn survivor patient who left him broken at the hospital. However, feeling despised, broken, and empty did not make Zacchaeus give up. He was longing for something higher and nobler that could heal and satisfy his heart. Jesus' attention to Zacchaeus gave him an opportunity to receive a spiritual miracle: the salvation that brought healing to him and his household.

Jesus wants us to bring the Gospel of healing and comfort to people who are rejected by society, are broken, and are hurt. I am so privileged and blessed to accept the fact that I am called from the highest place to go to the mission field to share the Gospel with the poor, the hurting, and the abandoned. I heard the call so clearly while in my dying state in the hospital, and I could not reject it. I was so excited to fulfill the calling, even though my wounds were still in the process of recovery, that I decided to go Oral Roberts University's seminary to be equipped, and I started ministry in a small church.

Like my colleague Zacchaeus, I left behind my work as a Chief Tax District person with no regret, and I was very blessed to welcome my destiny in Christ. Oh what a privilege to proclaim the Gospel to the world, and to take the healing news to the hurting. What Jesus did for Zacchaeus is an account of conversion from brokenness to a healed heart, which impacted his household and others. Zacchaeus was not afflicted by physical illness, but physical misery can cause brokenness. After meeting Jesus, Zacchaeus' brokenness was healed, which changed his attitude completely. When his life changed, then his family's lives and the lives of people around him changed, because he obeyed the voice from the highest place.

Chapter 10

WRITE YOUR STORY

*"Tell your children about it in the years to come,
and let your children tell their children. Pass the
story down from generation to generation"*
(Joel 1:3 NLT)

*"He has made everything beautiful in its time. He has
also set eternity in the hearts of men; yet they cannot
fathom what God has done from beginning to end"*
(Ecclesiastes 3:11)

We learned that the Japanese art of repairing broken pottery is called *kintsugi*. The philosophy behind the technique is to embrace the flawed and to keep the object, even after it is broken. This recognizes the history of the object. Through this art, the story of the piece of art of the object will be revealed. Damage is not the end of the object. *Kintsugi* is the story of an ugly broken object that was turned into a beautiful broken thing. The same thing can be true in life. An event that caused pain and brokenness is not the end of a life's story.

God is not done with you yet. Brokenness is part of the story of every human life in this world, and it does not need to be disguised. You have a story to write and to tell. It is like storytelling that is written in a journal or a book. As the storyteller, you can see your life in the chapter where the character goes through a series of pains, struggles, trials, tears, or joys. Whatever story you have, you need to make sure that your story will enrich you and others.

You may be reluctant to write your painful story, but do not be discouraged. Do not conceal your pain. The Bible reveals many painful stories of many people. It is true that the Bible is not just a story of success and victory. Rather, it is the complete story, including failure and pain. The Bible is the story of pain before a miracle takes place. It does not matter whether you have been healed, are in the process of being healed, or are enduring pain—your present life is a miracle in itself. If you have a story, then you had better expose it now. Your story will be an inspiration to read that others could benefit from, and that could bring glory to God. You never know whether your story might catch on like fire.

The Bible is the telling and retelling of the story of God. It is the story of the Creator in His creation, and vice versa. One of the stories is the narrative of how God saved the Israelites from their slavery in Egypt, and how this story was used by God to describe the coming of Christ Jesus to save the world from its slavery to sin. Much of God's truth is given in the context of story. The work of God in the lives of many people, and how people respond to it, is in the making of the story. The lives of Adam, Noah, Abraham, and Moses, and how they responded to God in their journeys are stories of humans and their Creator—and their stories were written in the Book of God. These stories help us trust God, know the character of God, and acknowledge God's work in our lives. We all have gone through many things in life, both pain and pleasure. We all have a story to tell, and the work of God in us informs our own life stories. Indeed, life is unfolding as stories that are worth telling.

God spoke to the prophet Jeremiah, "Write in a book all the words that I have spoken to you (Jer 30:2)." God gave the prophet Jeremiah His instructions to be a part of Israel's story in a book. The life story of Israel needed to be written according to God's instructions so that God would be pleased with it. As a result, Israel would be restored "'to the land I gave their ancestors to possess,' says the LORD (Jer 30:3)."

You see, Jeremiah was the one who penned the story, but God was the source of the story. You need to write your own story, but you must allow God to dictate it so that your story will be His story, and His story through your life will be the story that brings glory to His name. Your story shall turn to glory, and God is the only one qualified to direct your story. Journaling your daily activities is good but allowing yourself to be a vessel for God and to be an open book in your pain will display the Kingdom of God: His goodness and the grace of God to the world. Do not expose only your gain and hide your pain. Your pain is not your shame. You must write both as parts of your story. Paul encouraged us to,

" . . . Give thanks in all circumstances; for this is God's will for you in Christ Jesus (1 Thess 5:18)." Paul also said that we are open letters that are read by other people (2 Cor 3:2).

Your journal serves as a spiritual autobiography of you. Therefore, you must write it beautifully, honestly, and correctly so the reader of your story will be pleased with it. Trust God with your story, and do not write it on your own. When you write your story according to God's story, then your story will be good news to the world. The story of the woman who poured out an expensive perfume on the head of Jesus exposed her love to Jesus. She did a beautiful thing for Jesus, and this spread as good news of the Kingdom of God. Jesus said, "Truly I tell you, wherever this gospel is preached throughout the world, what she has done will also be told, in memory of her (Matt 26:10-13)." People will tell the story of this woman and remember her. God wants your willingness to be used in whatever way He sees fit. Let God write His unique story on your life. His story on your life is the ultimate act of submission to God.

When you submit your life to God, His Spirit will give you wisdom to enable you to write a beautiful story of your life, and you will be able to present it or to sing it out, like Fanny Crosby wrote in her song *Blessed Assurance*:

> Blessed assurance, Jesus is mine!
> O what a foretaste of glory divine!
> Heir of salvation, purchase of God,
> Born of His Spirit, washed in His blood.

This is my story, this is my song,
Praising my Savior all day long;
This is my story, this is my song,
Praising my Savior all day long.

Perfect submission, perfect delight!
Visions of rapture now burst on my sight;
Angels descending bring from above
Echoes of mercy, whispers of love.

Perfect submission—all is at rest,
I in my Savior am happy and blest;
Watching and waiting, looking above,
Filled with His goodness, lost in His love.[1]

Blessed Assurance is one of the thousands of hymns and about eight thousand poems that Fanny Crosby wrote.[2] She wrote these songs during much of her adult life. The fact that she was blind did not diminish her productivity, and many of these told who she was. She would formulate an entire song in her mind, and then she would dictate it to a friend or a secretary. She became blind at the age of six weeks from maltreatment of her eyes during a period of sickness. However, she lived to the age of 82.[3] Miss Fanny Crosby had the honor of being the first woman whose voice was heard publicly in the [United States] Senate Chamber at Washington.[4] Her handicap and hardship did not prevent her from expressing her gratitude to her Savior for who she is and writing her life story to present to her Creator. When asked about the secret of her contentment, she said that the following was the motto of her life:

> O what a happy soul am I!
>   Although I cannot see,
> I am resolved that in this world
>   Contented I will be;
>
> How many blessings I enjoy
>   That other people don't!
> To weep and sigh because I'm blind,
>   I cannot, and I won't.[5]

Fanny has brought comfort to many hearts and stirred up inspiration that will abide as long as life shall last.[6] Truly, Fanny's lack of vision did not keep her from writing her beautiful life story. She may have suffered from not seeing physically, but she was comforted emotionally, and she rose spiritually. Therefore, she had a beautiful story to tell to sufferers. The story you are writing may be in the middle of your pain, but it is going to be a beautiful story.

The Correcting Hand of the Author

Putting an idea on paper is not always easy. You may throw your concept into the rubbish several times. Then, you may rewrite it again and again until you find the correct idea. I remember that when I was working on my doctoral degree in seminary, my thesis was going back and forth, chapter by chapter, for months. A professor made a lot of corrections and revisions. Sometimes it was so frustrating, especially when I thought that my idea was brilliant, but the professor did not. I respected and accepted the more brilliant idea of my supervisor, and I agreed with it. From the introduction, through all the content, and up to my conclusion, they had to scrutinize it before they allowed me to defend it before the committee. I had to go through a scrutinizing process with my supervisor, which was very tiring, in order to perfect my thesis. However, this helped me defend it.

To write every chapter was tiring and time-consuming. What chapter are you in now, in your life? Are you too tired to write or inscribe the story of your life? Did you make many mistakes in the chapters of your life? Are you trying to avoid writing a difficult part of your story? Are you tired of being corrected? Do not worry. Keep writing your life story. It does not matter how far you go. Whether in the introductory chapter as a newborn believer, or in another content chapter as a long-time believer, you still have time to make corrections. You are not done yet. God is giving you a chance to rewrite your story. You will be able to write a beautiful conclusion to your story—and this is why you are still here now. If you allow the hand of the real Author, the real Supervisor, and the real Counselor, God's Spirit, to correct your mistakes, then you are on the right track. This is because the ultimate Author of life is always ready to help you beautify your story, no matter how many mistakes you have made.

Allow God to put His hand on your hand. Allowing God's hand means letting God write the story of your life according to His concepts and plan. When you allow His hand to guide and move your hand, then His hand becomes your hand, His mind becomes your mind, and you will be glad to declare, "I have the mind of Christ (1 Cor 2:16)." Because He guides you to write your story. Having the mind of Christ means allowing the plan, purpose, and perspective of Christ to be involved voluntarily in our actions. The mind of Christ is given to believers through the Spirit of God (1 Cor 2:10-12) to saturate their minds. When you put your faith in Christ into your spirit, then you also receive the mind of Christ. When faced with storms or hardships that require wisdom to handle, then you can trust in the mind of Christ to make the best decision. When you are struggling with your impure thoughts, then you can choose to let the mind of Christ control you (Phil 2:5). When you become one with God through His Spirit, then God will give you wisdom to enable you to write a beautiful story.

The story of my thesis going back and forth to the desk of my supervisor was a real experience. I was pleased that my supervisor made some corrections to perfect my paper. I made some mistakes, both intentionally and unintentionally. Mistakes were made intentionally because I thought they were the correct ideas. Mistakes were made unintentionally because I overlooked some things. All of these mistakes needed to be corrected. Thank God my supervisor was willing to point out the mistakes to be corrected. A lot of mistakes have been made in this life either intentionally or unintentionally, and because of these, sometimes we go through pain and suffering. However, do not worry—you have not finished your chapter yet. You are in the process of writing your story. It is okay to make some mistakes in life. No one is perfect. Mistakes are lessons for your good and your growth. Take a good lesson from these.

An illustration written by Dave Egner about a stubborn organist is interesting: A church organist was practicing playing some music created by Felix Mendelssohn, but he still could not play it properly. Annoyed, he then gathered up his music and was about to leave. He did not notice when someone had entered and sat in the back of the church. When the organist was about to leave, the person came forward and asked if he could play the piece. 'I never let anyone touch this organ!,' said the organist. After twice asking politely, finally the grumpy organist reluctantly allowed it. The person finally sat down and played beautiful perfect music that filled the church. When he finished, the organist asked, 'Who are you?' The man replied, 'I am Felix Mendelssohn.' The organist had almost prevented the song's creator from playing his own music! For a moment, the ego of the stubborn organist almost prevented his life from being corrected by the real creator and writer of the music.[7]

We, too, want to play the tones of our own lives according to our pattern, and we want to forbid our Creator from helping us play beautiful music with His skillful hands. In our inability, we often limit God's ability. Like the stubborn organist, we are often reluctant to allow the hands of the Master to correct our mistakes. Nevertheless, we are created in Christ Jesus to do good works, which God prepared in advance for us to do (Eph 2:10). Our lives cannot produce beautiful music with our limited abilities unless we allow the hand of God to work in us. God writes the symphony of our lives. Let Him do His work in your life. Our hands are too limited to play perfect music, and many times it causes the ears of the Master to hear the unpleasantness of our songs.

God made us to be His instruments. Some people have been endowed as musicians, song writers, singers, authors, or something else in other capacities. However, all must be done in harmony with the will of God. If any mistake is made, then be ready to make a correction to create a beautiful song for the Lord. Each capacity is a song of praise and worship to the Lord. Paul says, "Sing and make music from your heart to the Lord (Eph 5:19)." God desires music that comes from right hearts. Maybe our pain was one of God's ways to bring you back in tune with Him. Please allow His perfect hand to hold your hand, so that you can write a perfect song and story of life that are pleasing to God.

Like the stubborn organist, Peter, a disciple chosen by Jesus Himself, showed his impulsiveness and stubbornness to his Master by denying that he would ever deny Jesus when Jesus told His disciples that they would all fall away after He was arrested (Matt 26:33-35). Peter acted as though he knew his life better than Jesus, when it was the other way around. Peter should have said, "Help me, Lord, not to deny you."

Like the stubborn organist and Peter, we want to think that we know better than God and, therefore, we often go our own way. Do not create your own story just to make it look good—it is the story of God in you. There is nothing wrong with being bright and intelligent or educated. However, when we think that we know more than God, then we become ignorant to God's corrections. Fortunately, Jesus did not leave Peter alone when he made a mistake. Jesus was patient to correct Peter's attitude. Jesus forgave Peter and gave him another chance. God was not done with Peter, and He gave him another chance to write his story to please Jesus. To our amazement, at the end of the story when Jesus asked Peter whether he loved Jesus, Peter was able to say, "Lord, you know all things; you know that I love you (John 21:17)." When Peter was willing to receive correction, then he was ready to start a new beginning in his life, and Jesus was pleased with Peter and reinstated him.

When the content of your life story is excellent, then the conclusion of your life story will also be excellent. God will use your story to bring glory to Himself. God will glorify Himself in your life because it is not just your story—you are living the story of God in your life. Your story can turn out for the glory of God. Someday, someone, the real Author of life, will be happy to read the conclusion of your life story, and He will be ready to put His signature on it to endorse your story with one beautiful sentence: "Well done, my child, you did it, and I am well pleased with you."

Keep Writing—God is Not Done with You Yet

A book chapter usually consists of three parts: introduction, body, and conclusion. Putting your information into those three parts will help the reader understand the whole story that you are writing. You have your story to tell, and one part of it is your pain. However, do not stop in the middle of your pain—move on to the other side of your pain. There is another part of your life story that you must complete. Pain is not the end of your life story. There will a beautiful story to tell. This will be the way that God preserved you through pain. Your pain is a small part of a bigger picture of your life, but it will have a big impact on others if you include it in your story.

Joshua asked Israel to pass their stories on to the next generation when he told them, "Go over before the ark of the LORD your God into the middle of the Jordan. Each of you is to take up a stone on his shoulder, according to the number of the tribes of the Israelites, to serve as a sign among you. In the future, when your children ask you, 'What do these stones mean?' tell them that the flow of the Jordan was cut off before the ark of the covenant of the LORD (Josh 4:5-7).'" Memorial stones erected on the bank of the Jordan River provided an opportunity for parents to teach their children about the evidence of God's work in their lives. Through such teaching, it was hoped that the next generation always would remember the goodness and protection of God.

Joshua reminded Israel that their children would continue to be protected, even beyond the Jordan River, regardless of what the previous generation had gone through. The memorial stones recorded the stories of God's faithfulness in the wilderness up to the Jordan River, as well as the beginning of their victories beyond the Jordan River and into the Promised Land. Joshua had to remind the Israelites not to forget the good deeds of God—how God helped them as they wandered in the wilderness, as they crossed the Jordan River, and as they received what they were promised beyond the river.

Have you wandered long in the wilderness? Keep writing about what you have experienced in the wilderness. Soon it will be a story that preserves the evidence of God's work in you, and that will be of benefit to others. Every wilderness is the beginning of wellness, and every loss is a bridge to something else. There is always light at the end of the tunnel. God is not done with you yet. Keep on writing your story. Your mind may say that you are not good enough, but God never gives up on equipping you. He has rescued you to be His testimony, and He has given you time to complete His story in you. Your story is your identity that reflects who you are and where you have been.

The truth of the matter is that God is more interested in the bigger picture of your life. God wants to prove and perfect you through pain and suffering, and He is working on it. Let God do His part, and make yourself available, even as you go through trials. He is magnifying your true story so that hurting people will hear and will profit from it.

God has been patient with you, giving you a chance to live. There is a great potential inside you, and you must keep digging into it to a full extent in order to maximize your story. Each and every one of us is in the middle of writing our stories to mark our journeys. God is interested in your story because your story will be His story to bless and encourage others. Ann Kroeker suggests,

> Our stories, ultimately, aren't only about us; they're worthy of passing on because we can convey and validate God's faithfulness and goodness in our lives. People can hear our stories and respond not only with "You, too?" but also, "So that's how you got through. Maybe with God, I can get through, too." Whether we're telling stories of personal loss or of triumph in Christ, we can point people to God, taking every opportunity to share the good news of God's work in our lives. From core testimonies of repentance and salvation to everyday stories of struggle, hardship and hope, our lives reflect the grand story of God's work in this world.[8]

You may not be a good storyteller, but you may show others where God is in your story: both in your struggles and your gains. God will appreciate your openness in your story when you include God and reflect Him in it as the Author of your story. Do not hide your story. Keep writing and keep telling it. It is the work of God and the story of God engrafted in your life, in order for you to share them with the world. Your pain or healing story may create a connection with others who are facing pain like that through which God has carried you. When you share how God met you in that place, then you have created the door through which others may pass and find hope. The act of telling and retelling your story is a reminder of how God has been at work in you and through you. Your story is an open door for others, helping them see that they are not alone, creating courage to survive, and promoting sympathy for others. Life is a story. Keep writing your story and make your story a best-seller. Present it to God and sell it to others, no matter what chapter you are in. Let every chapter of your story be pleasing to God, and others will be blessed through it.

God Has Chosen You to Make a Story

When God has chosen you, then you are not going to be neglected. God never disappointed the ones He appointed. All of us are story-makers because life is a story. However, not many people want to make their stories come alive, but only preserve them as useless tombstones. Someday, all of us will have our own tombstones because God has chosen us to live on this earth. On these tombstones, sometimes you can see the dates of birth and the dates of death. The date of birth and the date of death were connected with a short line—a journey. It is a short line, but it tells your life story. Your family and friends will remember you by what kind of story you have made in the short line. The short line records a lot of stories.

Your story may be marked by some successes, but it will also be marked by some failures or pain. Nevertheless, let it be your legacy that can be alive in the hearts of your children, friends, and others. Jesus went through pain and suffering on the cross, died, and was buried in a tomb. Nevertheless, He lives today. His tomb is empty, and on the tombstone could have been written: "He is alive!" Jesus lives forevermore in the hearts of His followers. God has chosen you to make your story, marked by a short line, to be alive. The purpose of writing your story is not for a dead tombstone, but for a living stone that reflects the finished work of Christ in your life. You are a living stone (1 Pet 2:5) saved by God's love. David said, "Give thanks to the LORD, for He is good; his love endures forever. Let the redeemed of the LORD tell their story—those he redeemed from the hand of the foe (Ps 107:1-2)."

God has chosen you to experience pain, whether you are still struggling with it or have finished going through it. But you are still here. For this reason, David advises the redeemed to praise God. You gain confidence from every pain experienced, and this is the moment to share it. Your story is a living testimony to many who honor God.

The Scripture says, "For those God foreknew he also predestined to be conformed to the image of his Son (Rom 8:29)." You are called, under divine guidance, that every aspect of your life—even your pain—is to be a copy of Christ in this world.

Not all people are called to be full-time ministers like me. However, all of us can be the best disciples of Jesus as storytellers of God to the world. The Scripture tells us about people whom God chose and called for this specific purpose. The Old Testament speaks of people like Abraham, Moses, Samuel, Elijah, and others. The New Testament points out people like Peter and Paul, whom Jesus called. Church history also tells us about others who were called by God, like Augustine, Jerome, Justin Martyr, and Martin Luther.

A similar story in the 20th century was that of Corrie ten Boom, who resisted Nazi persecution, suffered internment in a concentration camp, and lost family members due to maltreatment in Nazi custody. Later, she became a world evangelist and motivational speaker, and she has been an encouragement to many people. Her autobiography cites her religious motivations that all human beings are equal before God. Oral Roberts, who suffered from severe tuberculosis, was used by God as a well-known evangelist for the healing ministry all over the world. Eric Liddell, who refused to run on Sunday because of his Christian faith, was disqualified from his original 100m distance at the Paris Olympics, but he won the 400m gold medal. Liddell's story an Oscar-winning film. Later in life, he became a missionary in China and inspired many people.

Many more people have been used by God in their unique stories to inspire millions of people. Their stories colored the real pictures of people's life journeys. Their stories were not autobiographies created to please people, and neither were they stories written on dead tombstones. Rather, their stories were about God in human beings to please God and to encourage others.

The stories of many people were written in the Bible, in church history, in books, or in magazines, but all were instrumental stories and became life stories that changed many lives. Like you and me, these chosen people went through pain and hardships. Their stories have been passed down to us, and we receive them as golden lessons in our time. We learn not only how they survived in their pain, but how their stories became the stories of books of life for people in our time and in future generations. The stories that they penned resonate with conviction and truth, encouraging millions of people.

Your story might not be as popular as theirs, but your story may impact others' lives: your family, your friends, or other communities. God can use your pain story, no matter how sad it is, and He can turn it into a beautiful healing story. You are called to proclaim and to demonstrate God's power in your pain. C. S. Lewis wrote, "God whispers to us in our pleasures, speaks in our conscience, but shouts in our pain."[9]

You have an important role to play in God's plan. Do not be shy to tell your story. Life is not about how much time you live, but how many lives you impact. Life becomes meaningful when it has an impact on other people. God has chosen you to be in your pain for a reason.

You have a voice, and you have a choice to make your story heard. After going through pain, hardship, and suffering, many people feel as though they failed and are defeated.

However, you succeeded and ascended and, therefore, you prevailed to be God's voice. Many people have tried hard in many ways in order to be heard. An athlete and an artist become famous because of their excellent talents. A successful businessman or businesswoman become known because of his or her riches. All these people have worked hard, and they celebrate their successes.

It is easy to celebrate life when you call it success, but not when you call it failure. It is easy to celebrate a life on the mountain top, but it is difficult to feast down in the valley. The world knows that it is easy to sing when nothing brings you down. It is easy to celebrate life, but not death. It is not easy to say that all is well when we are in trouble and pain. We all know that life has seasons. Fame, wealth, and health will only be temporarily. When it is all gone, then you do not have something to show and to present to the world. However, what God promises us is in Christ, which is far above anything that can be measured in earthly wealth, and God still has you and you have God. You have something to present to the world.

If you are in the valley of pain and trials, and others see you not frustrated but rejoicing, not weak but strong, not down but rising up, then people will be encouraged by it. When you cherish others, then you give yourself a chance to treat yourself well, because your good fruit comes from your own good tree. You are successfully impacting people by your lifestyle. People around you are watching how you react to your pain. They want to see if you are going to be sunk in the sand. They want to find out whether you are demoted or promoted through your pain.

Your actions have the power to bring healing and life-transformation to yourself and others. Your pain has the power to change the lives of others. Your story is for others to let them know that they are not alone. They want to hear from you.

You and I have been chosen by God to be the voices of the goodness of God to the suffering world. Make your story heard. Levi Lusko says, "Pain is a microphone. And the more it hurts, the louder you get. Suffering isn't an obstacle to being used by God. It is an opportunity to be used like never before."[10] When you make yourself available through your story, not only are others strengthened, but you will find yourself stronger than ever before. Lusko affirms,

> You have a stronger voice to project and to declare, and it's easier to belt from the diaphragm of your soul when you're hurting. It's counterintuitive, but in the middle of my hardest mess, I've found ministry to be a great strength waiting to be tapped into. It was welling up within me—a greater desire than ever before to tell the whole world that Jesus Christ can turn off the dark—because I experienced it myself. Right there, at ground zero, in the valley of the shadow of death. As hard as it was to claw our way through on hands and knees in those moments, I found

that when we poured our pain into ministry, whole new levels of usefulness opened up. There's perhaps no time you are as powerful as when you minister in the midst of pain.[11]

I have been sharing my story in churches, communities, on UChannel TV, and with the people I meet, and I will continue to do so. I want to encourage you, the sufferers, to arise, shine for your light has come, as Isaiah told it (Isa 60:1-6). Get up and shine your light. Color your story with bright colors so that others may see your story distinctively. Jesus said that He wants us to shine brightly, even when we feel that our light is dim.

It is my prayer that you will be willing to share your light wherever God put you. I pray that God, who has worked behind your story, will always get the credit for it, so that people who hear your story will say, "Ah, God has done it for him or her for a purpose." God has orchestrated things beautifully through pain. God has chosen you through your pain, and He strengthens you to bear the pain. However, you are not only a pain-bearer. You are a hope-bearer and a living testimony to the world. Christ in you is the hope of glory, and He wants you to impact the world. Your story has the power to bring healing to hurting people.

Thomson Mathew, a professional chaplain says this: "Positively impacting the people in our sphere of influence is the best way to lead others to a full knowledge of God."[12] Your story is a pulpit to the pews used by God, and someone is listening to your story attentively. Your godly actions can bring healing and wholeness to others. God wants you to change your world through your story. People like you, who have encountered afflictions, have been chosen to testify to this.

Share this hope with the world through your story. You are the main character of your own story. Better to live one story at a time, the story of God in you. Many people have been changed not by hearing a testimony of gain, but by hearing a testimony of pain and suffering like yours. I know that you do not like your pain. I do not either. However, it has been a changing life for me from bitter to better. It has shaped me to be a better person for the glory of God and a blessing for others.

NOTES

Prologue

1. Unless otherwise indicated, all Bible references in this book are to the New International Version (NIV) (Grand Rapids, MI: Zondervan, 2011).

Chapter 1: Wishing Life Would be Going Smoothly

1. Timothy Keller, *Walking with God through Pain and Suffering* (New York, NY: Riverhead Books, 2013), 2.
2. Keller, 2.
3. Wikipedia, "I Know that I Know Nothing," *Wikipedia.org*, 24 February 2020, https://en.wikipedia.org/wiki/I_know_that_I_know_nothing (accessed 28 March 2019).
4. David Jeremiah, *When Your World Falls Apart* (Nashville, TN: Word Publishing, 2000), 9.
5. Jeremiah, *When Your World Falls Apart*, 9.

6. Gordon MacDonald, *The Life God Blesses* (Nashville, TN: Thomas Nelson, 1997); quoted in Jeremiah, *When Your World Falls Apart*, 9.

7. MacDonald; quoted in Jeremiah, *When Your World Falls Apart*, 9.

Chapter 2: Pain and Suffering are Real

1. Jeremiah, *When Your World Falls Apart*, 33.

2. Francis Brown, S. R. Driver, and Charles A. Briggs, *A Hebrew and English Lexicon of the Old Testament* (Peabody, MA: Hendrickson Publishers, 1906), 1022.

3. C. H. Spurgeon, "Psalm 30," *Blue Letter Bible*, 5 December 2016, n.p., https://www.blueletterbible.org/Comm/spurgeon_charles/tod/ps030.cfm (accessed 21 April 2019).

4. William J. Petersen and Ardythe Petersen, *The Complete Book of Hymns* (Carol Stream, IL: Tyndale House, 2006), 303-304.

5. Petersen and Petersen, 303-304.

6. Jeremiah, *When Your World Falls Apart*, 33-34.

7. Jim Barbarossa, *Life Has Many Storms*, Real Life Stories, Lighthouse Edition 6 (Chesterton, IN: Lighthouse Christian Center, 2011), 75-78.

Chapter 3: Life is Full of Questions

1. Keller, 199.
2. Greg Laurie, "Why Did God Allow This to Happen?" *Harvest.org*, 2 October 2017, n.p., https://harvest.org/resources/gregs-blog/post/why-did-god-allow-this-to-happen/ (accessed 25 March 2019).
3. Laurie, n.p.
4. Keller, 26.
5. Laura Story with Jennifer Schuchmann, *When God Doesn't Fix It: Lessons You Never Wanted to Learn, Truths You Can't Live Without* (Nashville, TN: W Group, 2015), 141.
6. Bill Hamon, *Who am I and Why am I Here?* (Shippensburg, PA: Destiny Image Publishers, 2005), 89.

Chapter 4: You are Not Condemned

1. Sheila Walsh, *In the Middle of the Mess: Strength for This Beautiful, Broken Life* (Nashville, TN: Thomas Nelson, 2017), 24.
2. Walsh, 24.
3. Walsh, 157.
4. Thomas Watson, "Wise and Holy Sayings of Thomas Watson," *Gracegems.org*, n.d., n.p., https://gracegems.org/Watson/wise_and_holy_sayings.htm (accessed 16 May 2019).

Chapter 5: Pain is Essential

1. "Sense Organ," *Merriam-webster.com*, n.d., n.p., https://www.merriam-webster.com/dictionary/sense%20organ?utm_campaign=sd&utm_medium=serp&utm_source=jsonld (accessed 19 March 2020).

2. Associated Press, "Rare Disease Makes Girl Unable to Feel Pain," *Nbcnews.com*, 1 November 2004, n.p., http://www.nbcnews.com/id/6379795/ns/health-childrens_health/t/rare-disease-makes-girl-unable-feel-pain/#.XnO8X3IpA2w (accessed 2 July 2019).

3. David B. Curtis, "The Purpose of Pain—Hebrews 11:32-40," 22 March 2015, n.p., http://www.bereanbiblechurch.org/transcripts/hebrews/heb-11_32-40_purpose-of-pain.htm (accessed 20 June 2019).

4. Jeremiah, *When Your World Falls Apart*, 21-22.

5. Barbarossa, 26-28.

6. A. B. Simpson, *Christ in the Bible: James*, on *Swartzentrover.com*, 3 June 2010, n.p., http://swartzentrover.com/cotor/E-Books/holiness/Simpson/Commentary/James/James.pdf (accessed 30 July 2019).

7. David Jeremiah, *Overcomer: 8 Ways to Live a Life of Unstoppable Strength, Unmovable Faith, and Unbelievable Power* (Nashville, TN: W Publishing Group, 2018), 37.

8. Yan T. Wee, *In Silence, I Cry* (Singapore: Benjamin and Caleb Publisher, 2006), 1.

9. Wee, 1.

10. Tauren Wells, Emily Weisband, and Bernie Herms, "God's Not Done With You," *Azlyrics.com*, n.d., n.p., https://www.azlyrics.com/lyrics/taurenwells/godsnotdonewithyou.html (accessed 20 March 2020).

11. A. W. Tozer, *The Root of the Righteous* (Harrisburg, PA: Christian Publications, 1955), 137.

Chapter 6: What was Meant for Evil, but God Meant for Good

1. Lisa Bevere, *Be Angry but Don't Blow It: Maintaining Your Passion Without Losing Your Cool* (Nashville, TN: Thomas Nelson, 2000), 19.

2. TOW Project, "Job's Friends Blame Job for the Calamity (Job 4-23)," *Theologyofwork.org*, n.d., n.p., https://www.theologyofwork.org/old-testament/job/jobs-friends-blame-job-for-the-calamity-job-4-23 (accessed 20 March 2020).

3. TOW Project, n.p.

4. TOW Project, n.p.

5. Brown, Driver, Briggs, 966.

Chapter 7: You Can Be Whole Again

1. Stefano Carnazzi, "Kintsugi: The Art of Precious Scars," trans. Francesca Clemente, *Lifegate.com*, n.d., n.p., https://www.lifegate.com/people/lifestyle/kintsugi (accessed 17 July 2019).

2. Corrie Ten Boom; quoted in Linda Louk, *Sermon Notes Journal: Orange Sun Christian Inspirational Quotes* (N.p.: Createspace, 2019), cover.

3. Creflo Dollar, "Christ Will Restore Everything the Enemy Stole," *Creflo Dollar Ministries*, 30 July 2018, n.p., https://www.creflodollarministries. org/Daily-Devotionals/Weekly-Grace/Christ-Will-Restore-Everything-the-Enemy-Stole (accessed 17 October 2019).

4. John Gill, *John Gill's Exposition of the Bible*, on *Biblestudytools.com*, n.d., n.p., https://www.bible studytools.com/commentaries/gills-exposition-of-the-bible/deuteronomy-6-4.html (accessed 26 March 2020).

5. Mark D. Roberts, "Healing and the Kingdom of God," *Theologyofwork.org*, 16 May 2008, n.p., https://www.theologyofwork.org/the-high-calling/daily-reflection/healing-and-kingdom-god-0 (accessed 28 March 2020).

6. John Gill, *John Gill's Exposition of the Bible*, on *Biblestudytools.com*, n.d., n.p., https://www.bible studytools.com/commentaries/gills-exposition-of-the-bible/luke-9-2.html (accessed 26 March 2020).

7. Dale Fletcher, "John Wesley on Holistic Health and Healing," *Faithandhealthconnection.org*, 28 October 2010, n.p., https://www.faithandhealth-connection.org/john-wesley-holistic-health-and-healing-interview-by-randy-maddox/ (accessed 26 March 2020), with quotations from from Deborah Madden, "Introduction: Saving Souls and Saving Lives; John Wesley's 'Inward and Outward Health,'" in *'Inward and Outward Health': John Wesley's Holistic Concept of Medical Science, the Environment and Holy Living*, ed. Deborah Madden (London: Epworth, 2008), 4.

8. Oral Roberts, *Healing for the Whole Man* (Tulsa, OK: Oral Roberts Evangelistic Association, 1965), 12.

Chapter 8: Make Your Test Becomes Your Testimony.

1. Bevere, 16.
2. Jeremiah, *When Your World Falls Apart*, 9.
3. A. J. Russell, *God Calling* (Uhrichsville, OH: Barbour Books, 1998), June 22.
4. James R. Sherman, *Rejection* (Golden Valley, MN: Pathway Books, 1982), 45.
5. Christine Caine, *Undaunted: Daring to Do What God Calls You to Do* (Grand Rapids, MI: Zondervan, 2012), 105.
6. Caine, 108.
7. Caine, 109-123.

8. John Henry Jowett, on *Goodreads.com*, n.d., n.p., https://www.goodreads.com/quotes/809966-god-does-not-comfort-us-to-make-us-comfortable-but (31 March 2020).

9. Wee, 20.

10. T. D. Jakes, *Daily Readings from Crushing: 90 Devotions to Reveal How God Turns Pressure into Power* (New York, NY: Hachette Book Group, Inc., 2019), "Comforted to Comfort", 4-5.

Chapter 9: Live a Radical Life for Christ

1. Van Johns, *Living Beyond Survival: Laughing, Loving, Sharing...Life!* (Bloomington, IN: Author House, 2011), 59.

2. Johns, 54.

3. American Trauma Society, "Jason's Story," *Trauma Survivors Network*, n.d., n.p., https://www.trauma-survivorsnetwork.org/pages/1148 (accessed 27 July 2019).

4. David Platt, *Radical: Taking Back Your Faith from the American Dream* (Colorado Springs, CO: Multnomah Books, 2010), 183.

5. Platt, 184.

6. Platt, 21.

7. Dietrich Bonhoeffer, *The Cost of Discipleship* (New York: Macmillan, 1959), 43-44.

8. Bonhoeffer, 44.

9. Bonhoeffer, 45.

Chapter 10: Write Your Story

1. Petersen and Petersen, 94.
2. Jacob H. Hall, "Miss Fanny J. Crosby: Hymn Writer and Poetess," *Wholesomewords.org*, n.d., n.p., https://www.wholesomewords.org/biography/bcrosby5.html (accessed 11 July 2019).
3. Hall, n.p.
4. Hall, n.p.
5. Hall, n.p.
6. Hall, n.p.
7. David C. Egner, "God's Song," in *Great is Thy Faithfulness: 365 Devotions from Our Daily Bread* (Grand Rapids, MI: Discover House, 2009), February 10.
8. Ann Kroeker, "What's Your Story?" *By Faith Magazine*, 18 May 2016, n.p., https://byfaithonline.com/whats-your-story/ (accessed 17 July 2019).
9. C. S. Lewis, *The Problem of Pain* (1940; reprint San Francisco: HarperCollins, 2001), 91.
10. Levi Lusko, *Through the Eyes of a Lion: Facing Impossible Pain, Finding Incredible Power* (Nashville: W Publishing Group, 2015), 108.
11. Lusko, 113-114.
12. Thomson K. Mathew, *What Will your Tombstone Say?* (Maitland, FL: Xulon Press, 2008), 199.